What's a Parent to Do?

Straight Talk
on Drugs and Alcohol

What's a Parent to Do?

Straight Talk
on Drugs and Alcohol

Henry David Abraham, M.D.

New Horizon Press
Far Hills, New Jersey

Dedication

This book is dedicated to the thousands of kids, the ones who made it and the ones who didn't, and their families whom I have been privileged to treat over the years. They have humbled me with their suffering, inspired me with their courage and cheered me with their victories.

New Horizon Press
P.O. Box 669
Far Hills, NJ 07931

Henry David Abraham, M.D.
What's a Parent to Do?
Straight Talk on Drugs and Alcohol

Cover Design: Robert Aulicino
Interior Design: Susan M. Sanderson

Library of Congress Control Number: 2004108080

ISBN: 0-88282-238-1
New Horizon Press

Manufactured in the U.S.A.

2008   2007   2006   2005   2004   /   5   4   3   2   1

Table of Contents

Foreword

I write this book as a specialist in drug abuse, a psychiatrist and a parent. *What's a Parent to Do?* has three goals above all others — to empower parents to prevent drug abuse in their kids, to give parents and their kids the latest medical knowledge about the drugs that are common in our schools and on our streets and to help parents help their children find their way back if drugs become a problem in their lives.

In my thirty years of work with kids and their parents, one problem I've run into too often is the knowledge gap between parents and children when drugs are at issue. It's like they are living on separate planets without the benefit of telephones. Often neither the kids nor their loved ones have a complete, or even helpful, handle on drugs as danger. Each group knows things the other does not. Kids on the edge of testing the waters of drug use get their information from friends. Kids already abusing drugs see no problem with drug use or feel helpless to stop. Parents get their information from newspapers, television or the hazy memories of their own teen years. They usually can see the consequences of drug craziness in their kids, but are often in the dark about their children's motivations to use drugs, how to prevent it or how to help them once real trouble begins.

When the child is a teenager, this knowledge gap can narrow if there is openness about drugs and drug abuse in the family. More often the gap between parent and child is covered over with denial. If a child is to embark on a career in drug abuse, more often than not it begins in the teen years. But kids are seldom open about drug use and the warning signs to parents are subtle. Trouble may be present, but it is often invisible or dealt with on a don't-ask-don't-tell basis until tragedy comes knocking. Trouble at this stage is likely to be not so much a wake-up call as the siren of an ambulance. At this point, parents are often too shell-shocked to know what action is best. In the meantime, the teen, if he is still mobile, continues to tiptoe into the toxic waters of drug abuse, trying to keep it a covert operation and all the while claiming that "everything is cool." I want to give parents the tools they need to take action when things aren't so cool. In particularly troubled situations, a kid will start using drugs before the teen years or carry them over into troubling behavior afterwards. This book is for parents of these kids, too.

Not everything you hear about drugs is true. Modern equivalents of *Reefer Madness*, the anti-marijuana propaganda film of the thirties, abound today, but on both sides of the debate over drug use and abuse. Marijuana and Ecstasy enthusiasts dismiss reports of medical complications from those drugs as propaganda. Governmental authorities continue to punish drug-involved kids with penalties more severe than those for homicide, rape and robbery. Where is the balance in all this?

Recent evidence shows that costly programs aimed at teaching drug abstinence in elementary schools appear to be lost causes by the time the children reach high school. The paradoxical consequence of such programs may be to pathologize normal curiosity and limit testing in kids, increase their curiosity about drugs and devalue what adults have to say. On a happier note, the majority of kids using drugs do not graduate to careers in addiction. Indeed, some data show that teenage drug experimenters may be psychologically healthier than abstainers or frequent users, an apparently valid finding which gets little discussion in the smoke and mirrors of public debate.

One goal for *What's a Parent to Do??* is to narrow this attitude gap between parent and child, family and victim and to facilitate talk without hysteria. I hope that I can open the drug dialogue between parent and child, whether the discussion is theoretical or crisis-driven. If a conversation about drugs is not to become like talking to a wall, a parent needs to see the problem from the kid's point of view and the kid needs to know the same set of facts as his or her parents, insofar as that is possible. There is no substitute for a parent (or teen, for that matter), standing on firm clinical and scientific ground when taking on the problem of drugs and drug effects. This book tries to give you that grounding.

This book is also for parents worried about kids who are at risk for using drugs, whether because of their friends, environment or the track record of older siblings, but who show no signs that this is happening yet. What we've learned in the past thirty years of work is that a parent can both detect trouble before it happens *and prevent it*. Experimentation with drugs tends to begin in junior high school, expand in high school and solidify then into patterns of abuse and addiction. Thus, for a prevention strategy to work, knowledge of what to expect and what to do about it is essential.

Although the audience for this book is parents, I hope that what's in it will tempt more than one kid to peek over her parent's shoulder from time to time. To that end, leaving the book in plain sight, preferably near a television set or by a warm bowl of popcorn is a better strategy than wrapping it in brown paper. This book can be a resource for kids in high school and college dealing with the dangerous and deadly nonsense that passes for knowledge about drug use among peers. *What's a Parent to Do?* can also serve as a resource for counselors and teachers of drug abuse programs for those students. It's not my goal to offer a scholarly or encyclopedic view of the field. This is not a textbook. The typical text in psychiatry nowadays is written by a platoon of specialists summarizing the research of an army of scientists. While this mass of knowledge represents admirable clinical, pharmacological and social advances that have been made dealing with drugs and drug abuse, its scientific depth usually does not address the specific needs of parents who are trying to prevent drug abuse in their kids or who must make life and death decisions if their kids cross that line.

This book is intended to help parents with precisely those problems. *What's a Parent to Do?* is not intended to be a bag of sure-fire tricks that parents can use on their kids. There is no magic to good parenting or to preventing and treating drug abuse. But it's my hope that *What's a Parent to Do?* is a concise, clear summary of the tried, the true and the best stuff on the horizon — biological, psychological and societal. My hope is that people, after reading this book, will be able to answer questions like, "What is Ecstasy? What is crack? How is it different from cocaine? And what about anabolic steroids?" Or "How does a parent prevent her kid from getting involved in drugs in the first place?" and "How can I help a kid who is in drug trouble?" The last question is particularly important, because when parents can answer that, they are on the road to empowerment over a problem that now threatens our families and society.

What's a Parent to Do? is an effort to translate the technical and the controversial into practical facts of easy accessibility and use. In the interest of readability, individual points in the text are not referenced; the information is intended for rapid access and use. This book is about kids who have fallen into difficulties with drugs, or are at risk to do so. They are of both genders. When it is useful to use the third person singular pronoun, this book uses it nonspecifically unless the context dictates otherwise. Case histories arise from clinical experiences and published reports. Anonymity of patients and their families has been maintained by the avoidance of potential identifiers or the presentation of a given clinical example as the composite of multiple cases. I have done this to respect the confidentiality of my patients and their families and to telescope important clinical information into a more efficient presentation. The points are not intended to be exaggerated, exhaustive or equivocating. Inaccuracies are solely the author's responsibility. I welcome being told about them.

The book is organized into three parts: what you need to know about street drugs *before* your kid gets involved; what the drugs are; and what to do if you have to deal with the problems of a kid who abuses or is addicted to drugs. Chapter 1, "The Terrible, Horrible, No-Good World of Drugs" describes basic concepts in what drugs are, how they work, what kids use and which are more dangerous. Chapter 2, "Kids at Risk: Do Genes Matter?" describes genetic factors that increase a child's risk of drug abuse. Chapters 3 and 4, "Heads-Up Parenting: Red Flags and Golden Haloes" and "Prevention, the Best Treatment," describe ways in which a parent can predict and influence a kid's risk of future drug use. For the majority of parents, this is essential reading. These two chapters are about stitch-in-time parenting. When it's applied, lifetimes of pain and heartache can be avoided. Please, read these two chapters very carefully. They contain the solution to our drug epidemic: informed parents taking effective action. Chapter 5, "What the Three Pigs Can Teach You about Drug Abuse," is for the reader who wants to be able to dig in more deeply and draw his or her own conclusions from the medical literature.

Chapters 6 through 15 cover specific drugs or drug classes: what the drugs are, how they work, what they do to you and discussions of drug-specific treatments for such problems as overdoses, withdrawals and addictive states.

Chapter 16, "Tips for Parenting the Saturday Night Adventurer," discusses how a parent should approach the kid who is just sticking his toe in the waters of drug abuse. Chapter 17, "How to Manage an Overdose," can be the most important chapter in this book for some families for obvious reasons. The good news is that the majority of individuals suffering drug overdoses coming to the emergency room live to tell the tale. Chapter 18 addresses a painful issue, "When Kids Are Addicts." Chapter 19, "Double Trouble: the Dually Diagnosed Kid," deals with kids carrying two burdens, a drug-related diagnosis and another psychiatric diagnosis such as depression or psychosis. These kids have *special handling* stamped all over them. The chapter describes the problems they have and solutions that work. The last chapter, "How to Make This Epidemic History," covers the problem of drug abuse both as a preventable and treatable social disorder, with specific recommendations for you to help reverse the madness.

Contrary to what is common in other popular books on drug abuse, there is no glossary of drug slang appended to this book. In my third of a century of work with drug abusers and their families, I simply have never known of a meaningful intervention which came about from a parent's knowledge of drug slang. Even knowledge of the specific type of drug being abused is not always helpful to a parent. Who is the parent who will take comfort in the fact her daughter is only shooting ketamine and not heroin? Yet the knowledge about which drug classes are potentially fatal on withdrawal is clearly worth having.

I hope that this book adds to a parent's critical thinking about drug use. It's important not only for one's credibility in discourse, but because street drugs *do* carry dangers, both for the time of their use and for years afterwards. The dangers are from what drugs do to one's brain, behavior, livelihood and relationships. And as those who argue for legalization of marijuana point out, there is danger from a society that converts drug users into criminals instead of recognizing them as victims or adventurers of the mind. In the debate over drug use in society, often the borders between drug use, drug abuse and drug addiction are blurred. But each is quite distinct from the others. Use is not abuse and abuse is not addiction. Thus, learning the dangers of street drugs, the real ones, is essential for the survival and health of millions of kids and their families.

Finally, I hope that this book will offer direction for help to parents before their kids use drugs or when they are using and before they wade too deeply into trouble. I also want parents to know what to do during a drug crisis or after it has occurred. Even a drug crisis like an emergency room visit or criminal arrest can offer a rare and important opportunity for intervention. And last, I want to share the experience of this field regarding drug abstinence, harm reduction and, most importantly, the steps needed for the road back. There can be an end to addiction. Treatment works. This is the mantra that needs to be shouted from the highest rooftops. It's not easy, not foolproof and recovery is not always for keeps, but treatment is important, effective and vastly better than punishment. Now is the time for moms and dads to tackle the dangers of drug abuse, the real dangers and fight the good fight for our children.

Part I

What Parents Need to Know NOW: So Your Kid Won't Head Down the Slippery Path of Drugs and Alcohol

Chapter 1

The Terrible, Horrible, No-good World of Drugs

"If all the drugs in the world fell into the sea, it would be all the better for mankind and all the worse for the fishes."

-Introductory lecture on pharmacology to medical students at the Johns Hopkins University School of Medicine

What Drugs Are for Real

Mom, Dad, let's not mince words. Drugs are poisons. Let's call a poison any agent which, when given to a living thing, especially in a small amount, hurts or kills it. This applies to the vast majority of little bottles in your medicine cabinet. Aspirin can act as a poison as much as, if not more so, than morphine. To be fair, poisons that are carefully researched and tested within specific clinical guidelines for the treatment of human suffering we also call medications.

Besides pharmaceuticals used incorrectly, there are other poisons to consider. These are produced without pharmaceutical and governmental standards, without proof of human safety and efficacy, and which are used for alterations of mental function. These are street drugs. By this definition, heroin and cocaine are street drugs. So are alcohol and tobacco, despite the fig leaf of governmental regulation which covers them with legality. This is because they are toxic to humans and serve no proven clinical purpose.

The science of pharmacology, which studies the effects of drugs on living things, grew out of the science of toxicology, the study of the poisoning of living things. Ancient Greeks saw only dangers in drugs. The earliest compounds studied at the dawn of pharmacology in the nineteenth century were the poisons curare and strychnine. Medicinal chemistry grew from that point, spawned by the development of organic chemistry. It is likely that the science of toxicology itself grew from observations made over time by hunter-gatherers before the invention of agriculture.

Drug Epidemic

So what's the big deal? Kids know that drugs can kill you, that HIV comes from sharing needles (or unprotected sex), even that boozing runs in families. But if kids are so smart, why do they take chances with drugs and alcohol? What puts them at risk and how big is the risk in the first place? Is there a true drug epidemic? What is the harm in a little drug experimentation? How about the argument that street drugs can be beneficial? Or that the government has drug abuse under control? The Federal government spends billions spritzing foreign soil with herbicides, supplying foreign armies with jet fighters and anti-aircraft missiles and training sniffer dogs for drug screening in Tijuana and Nogales. Drug felons are captured in increasing numbers, making prison development by some measures America's number one growth industry. Sadly, all this has the makings of a lose-lose game, bad for the felons, bad for the rest of us who foot the bill. Drugs continue to pour Niagara-like into the United States.

Despite all they're told, our kids continue to doubt the warnings of adults and continue to experiment. Many try and too many regularly use drugs. In some ways, kids are volunteers without parental permission in a vast, uncontrolled experiment with mind-altering drugs. But the research agenda of our kids is different from that of the National Institute on Drug Abuse.

Many kids want to find out if a drug is fun. At what dose and by which route? Are there side effects? And often as an afterthought, is it safe? In the back of their minds kids may see drugs as helping them "get through the day," but not specifically helping with depression, anxiety or difficulties concentrating in school. Occasionally an especially bright kid will argue that drug use will make you more creative. A few words about this idea.

Do Drugs Make You Creative?

No, drugs make you high and sometimes they make you addicted or crazy. That's the short answer. A more eloquent answer comes from novelist John Lanchester writing in the *New Yorker* magazine in 2003. In his article, he analyzed the best written works of famous writers on and off various drugs. Psychedelic means, after all, "mind manifesting." So where were all the literary manifestations of drug-using writers? Writers on speed (Graham Greene, Jean-Paul Sartre, Philip K. Dick, W.H. Auden) produced prodigious work, though much of Sartre's incoherence is surely attributed to drug intoxication. Often, too, the paranoia of speed crept into the work or in Dick's case, roiled through his brain. Writers who wrote about drugs (William Burroughs' *Naked Lunch*, Aldus Huxley in *The Doors of Perception*) often used them. Lanchester concludes, "...these books are worth reading — but no one could pretend that drugs have given us anything resembling a canon of major writing." In the field of popular music, those who were abusers have often lived lives that ended in disaster (Janis Joplin, Kurt Cobain, Andy Gibb).

Our Kids Are in an Uncontrolled Experiment

This children's crusade of drug experimentation is not science as much as social enterprise. That's because the usual mechanisms one puts in place to measure a drug's effect, such as control groups, fixed doses, pure drugs and reliable outcome measures, are absent. In their place are the whims of teenagers, governed by less predictable factors like peer pressure, opportunity, drug supply and cost and multiple others detailed later in this book.

Each year since 1975 The Institute for Social Research at the University of Michigan has conducted a survey of as many as 45,000 American high school students regarding their use and attitudes towards drugs. Table 1 shows drugs 13,300 high school seniors have used at least once in their lifetimes. Half have used "an illicit drug." Almost half have used marijuana. One in seven has used a hallucinogen like LSD. One in ten has used a club drug like Ecstasy. Almost as many have tried cocaine. 80 percent have drunk alcohol and over 60 percent have tried cigarettes. According to this survey, half of our children are involved in drug crimes by their own admission. Nearly two thirds of our children are flirting with nicotine addiction. These drugs operate on the brain with powerful effects, in small quantities, with long-term effects on mental and social function and direct and indirect lethality. In fact, two-thirds of all violent crimes occur under the influence of alcohol or drugs. Table 1 highlights a study in 2003 of what drugs high school students have reported trying by their senior year.

TABLE 1: What Drugs High School Seniors Have Used by the Year 2003

Drug	Using in Lifetime
Alcohol	76.6 %
Cigarettes	53.7 %
Any Illicit Drug	51.1 %
Marijuana	46.1 %
Amphetamines	14.4 %
Inhalants	11.2 %
Hallucinogens	10.6 %
Barbiturates	8.8 %
Ecstasy	8.3 %
Cocaine	7.7 %
Anabolic Steroids	3.5 %
PCP	2.5 %
Heroin	1.5 %

The numbers tell only part of the story. The current epidemic of drug use strikes hard at our young. But the human faces behind these numbers are all too often lost in the rush to make policy, sell drugs, protect markets or placate lobbies. Why do kids use drugs? How bad is this epidemic? Which drugs and drug behaviors are more worrisome? And most importantly, what can we do to protect our kids? To answer these questions, we have to overcome several large obstacles: the effects of drug marketing to our kids and ourselves; our own attitudes and information about drugs; the effects of drug misinformation in dialogue with our kids; and most essentially, the sense of despair that nothing can be done to solve these problems in the first place.

How Drugs Work in the Brain: Cliffs Notes Version

Without doubt the human brain is the most complex matter in the universe. It's the brain's job to keep the body out of trouble and to get work done. The simplest "brain" is a pair of neurons, or nerve cells, doing separate jobs. One cell senses what's going on in the environment. The other takes action. This primitive nervous system found in the sea snail, Aplysia, has provided a treasure trove of insight into basic brain mechanisms and has led to one Nobel Prize in Medicine so far, with more likely to be on the way. The importance of this work is that it provides insights into a microcosm of how the human brain works.

The human brain, of course, is far more complex than a sea snail's (with occasional exceptions). The typical human brain consists of billions, yes, billions, of neurons packed together and wired in complexity. Brain cells throughout the animal kingdom serve similar biological ends: to scope out the environment and then decide what to do about it. The sea snail may withdraw if it's shaken up, not too differently from a swimmer who flees at the sight of a shark. In the human's case, however, the decision to call it a day and make for dry land comes from a far more complicated set of mental activities involving perception, memory, reasoning and motor action. The problem is that drugs and alcohol affect all of these, for the most part, adversely.

Brain cells coordinate mental activity by communicating with one another using small molecules, neurotransmitters, which float from one cell to another through a tiny sea of salt water called a synapse (forgive me if I am repeating a biology class you remember with fear and trembling, but press on). There are more synapses in the brain than stars in our galaxy. A transmitter molecule such as serotonin may move en masse between neurons with the message, "Chill out, dude!" with the result that a person feels less anxious or depressed.

Drugs can interfere with this communication between neurons in one of two general ways. A drug can alter the amount of the neurotransmitter from the transmitting neuron, as cocaine does, or it can operate on the receiving neuron to enhance or block a neurotransmitter's natural effects. A drug may artificially increase a neuron's action at a receptor. This is how a narcotic like morphine works, increasing the brain's ability to block out pain, create a high and possibly stop you from breathing. Drugs that operate the same way as chemicals ordinarily found in the body are called agonists. Other drugs may work by doing the opposite, block the effects of agonist drugs and the natural chemicals they imitate. These blockers are called antagonists. The drug naloxone is a good example of an antagonist. It blocks the effects of narcotics and is useful in the emergency treatment of narcotic overdoses.

Another way a drug may act is by doing part of the job a neurotransmitter does. The hallucinogen LSD is thought to work this way. It acts like serotonin, an important neurotransmitter for regulating mood, sleep, appetite and sexual function, at specific brain receptors. It is important to note that while we can often explain how a drug operates at a molecular level and can sometimes do the same at the level of the neuron, we are deeply humbled when we try to explain a drug's effect on the behavioral level. This is because a single drug nearly always affects many different kinds of neurons and each neuron in turn connects with gazillions more. So, anyone claiming to know precisely how a drug changes a person's behavior has a lot of explaining to do.

How Drugs Are Dangerous

Drugs operate with powerful effects in small quantities. They have long-term effects on mental and social function and direct and indirect lethality. If all drugs are poisons, you may ask, why are they made, sold and used with ever increasing enthusiasm? The answer is straightforward. Drugs are dangerous depending on their dose, route of administration and the peculiar vulnerabilities of the person using them. Regulating these factors can make most drug use relatively safe. Dose appears to be the major factor in drug related harm.

The route of administration is another source of danger to the user. It is safest not to use heroin at all, less safe to inhale it, but least safe to shoot it intravenously, since the last case exposes the user to contracting HIV and hepatitis C, two often-fatal illnesses. Not every person given a narcotic becomes a narcotics addict. Why is that? The answer is one of the most important questions in the study of addictions. An important factor likely to explain differences in addiction potential between people is differences in genetic vulnerability. The research on alcohol dependence is particularly convincing in this respect, showing how alcoholism runs in families, even after taking into account the effects of environment. And so, in addition to dose and route, genetic vulnerability to a particular drug increases one's danger.

However, vulnerability may not only be a genetic phenomenon, but an environmental one as well. Building up tolerance to a drug confers a certain resistance to the drug in the experienced user. This requires using more of the drug more frequently, a clear-cut sign that drug dependence is developing. The good news in this case is that tolerance lessens the chance of a fatal overdose, since the user's body breaks the drug down more efficiently, or otherwise protects itself better. The Tsarist monk Rasputin protected himself from arsenic poisoning by taking small doses of the drug daily to build tolerance. The strategy worked: after his royal employers failed to poison him, they had to beat, shoot and throw him into the freezing Neva to finish the job.

When a drug is taken in a large dose or when a young person is especially sensitive, disaster is likely, in the form of direct damage to the brain, heart or lungs, resulting in seizures, asphyxia, heart failure, coma and death. Most dangerous is when more than one drug is used simultaneously, e.g., heroin and alcohol. Both drugs suppress breathing, but in different parts of the brain, making the result much more profound. This is called drug *synergy*. The accidental overdoses of certain rock stars and movie idols are often associated with synergy. The comic genius John Belushi, for example, is thought to have died from a combination of cocaine and heroin, a practice commonly referred to on the street as speedballing. Similarly, singer Janis Joplin died from a combination of alcohol, heroin and marijuana; another musician, Jimi Hendrix, died from alcohol and barbiturates.

Dysfunction and death are not limited to the rich and famous. Average kids are especially vulnerable. One such young person who later came to me for treatment was Bill T. Bill was everything his loving parents could want in a teenage son—a bright student, co-captain of the football team and blessed with a raft of friends. He was on a trajectory towards an Ivy League education and a career in medicine like his older sister. He had experimented with marijuana on the occasional weekend in his sophomore year of high school and, seeing himself as an adventurer of the mind, had tried LSD three times. The trips were fun. He saw kaleidoscopic colors and shapes. Music in particular seemed richer and more meaningful. He laughed a great deal. The paranoid fear that he was being televised as he tripped the third time lasted only a few moments. He was left feeling animated and refreshed the next morning. Occasionally in the weeks that followed, he would notice afterimages of objects as they passed through his line of sight. On advice of friends, he decided to trip a fourth time, on the theory that another LSD trip would help him "complete" the last one and get rid of the persisting trails he was seeing.

The fourth trip did not cure Bill's afterimages. In fact, following the trip the trailing afterimages came daily. Worse, the euphoric feeling of his previous trips returned, but then degenerated into a merely annoying buzz he could not shake. One evening lying in his bed, he listened to a favorite rock and roll station before sleep. The rest of the family had gone to bed. He heard the punk group, The Clash. But there was one problem that puzzled him. The radio, like the rest of the house, was dark. Bill's radio was off. Yet over and over he heard the refrain, "Should I stay or should I go now?" He couldn't sleep. In fact, he felt energized. A thought popped into his head: His ability to hear The Clash was because he had received a gift from God. The President of the United States needed to know this. Bill was going to get the Medal of Honor. He would fly to Washington to tell the President. Bill rose from his bed, dressed and slipped out the door into the night. And so began Bill's career as a man with psychosis, which, despite my best efforts, remained life-long until his death by suicide.

Not all drug use is equally dangerous. Drugs vary widely in many physical and mental effects. Consider a piece by Jane Brody in *The New York Times* in 2004, in which she cites a ranking by the Institute of Medicine of the addiction potential of various drugs: 9 percent of people who try marijuana become dependent on it, compared to 32 percent of those who try cigarettes. Heroin and cocaine fall in between those numbers.

Taking a hint from the star rating systems for restaurants and movies, one can construct a table of comparative drug worries. Table 2 ranks drugs according to my Clinical Worry Index, which is based on direct and indirect lethality, emergency room visits, long term effects, addictive potential, social availability and comorbid illnesses, that is, the illnesses that often come along with the use of a particular drug. Evidence supporting this ordering is detailed in subsequent chapters dealing with each drug or drug class. Some may take issue with my ranking, since such a scheme is arguable at best. For example, it is well known that sedative drugs like barbiturates are often lethal in overdoses. However, tens of thousands more people will die this year from cigarette related deaths than barbiturates. This argues strongly, to my way of thinking, for rating tobacco as more dangerous. And the Index does not in any way argue that some drugs on the list, such as marijuana or anabolic steroids, are "safe."

No drugs are safe. They are only useful if the good they do outweighs the potential harm. The Index only says that drugs rated with fewer skulls are socially *less dangerous* than drugs with more. If a drug lower on the scale were to be abused in more dangerous ways, or if the drug attracted more kids, or if a new problem were discovered about the drug, one could imagine its status rising on the Worry Index. The opposite it also true. That is, a new drug danger may appear on the horizon, but still not compare to drugs freely available to kids. A case in point is Oxycontin, a helpful oral narcotic painkiller which addicts have learned to inject and for which some addicts even kill pharmacists. Despite Oxycontin's deadly impact on two fronts, the numbers of its victims remain dwarfed by those lives ruined by tobacco-related cancers and alcohol-related carnage on our highways.

TABLE 2: Parents Guide to Dangerous Drugs:
            Clinical Worry Index

DRUG	COMPARATIVE DANGER
Tobacco	☠️ ☠️ ☠️ ☠️
Alcohol	☠️ ☠️ ☠️ ☠️
Heroin	☠️ ☠️ ☠️
Amphetamines	☠️ ☠️ ☠️
Cocaine	☠️ ☠️ ☠️
PCP	☠️ ☠️ ☠️
Inhalants	☠️ ☠️ ☠️
Hallucinogens	☠️ ☠️
Anabolic steroids	☠️ ☠️
Marijuana	☠️
Sedatives	☠️

The Drug Business

A significant obstacle to dealing with the drug epidemic is the effect of drug marketing on our kids and ourselves. Drugs are everywhere. Lawful drugs comprise an international multi-billion-dollar business. The largest drug manufacturer, Merck, has a market capitalization of $142 billion dollars, a sum larger than the gross national products of the majority of the nations of the world. Unlawful drugs also comprise a huge international business, but by its nature its financial reach is harder to estimate. Legal and illegal, the production, marketing and distribution of drugs arise from formidable economic machinery that is global in voice, appeal and influence.

In fairness, pharmaceutical manufacturers have in many ways been pioneers for a revolution in medical breakthroughs. Prescription drugs can now regulate our hearts, blood pressure, mood and stomach acid. Where our ancestors suffered short, painful lives, people today have the chance to expect long, health, comfortable lives, in large measure because of pharmacological advances.

On the other hand, the marketing of drugs to doctors and patients has become increasingly aggressive. It is rare to find an advertisement from a drug company that does not feature an image of an attractive model brimming over with gratification for the drug product. Companies have long spent money on advertising over-the-counter drugs. Similarly, the "recreational" drugs alcohol and tobacco are aggressively marketed today despite efforts of government controls dating back to Columbus' time. Despite recent legal settlements in the billions of dollars between American tobacco companies and several states, the makers of Camel and Newport cigarettes persist in targeting the young in print ads in *Rolling Stone, Sports Illustrated* and *TV Guide.*

A new and particularly popular technique among over-the-counter drug marketers that has been adopted by prescription drug manufacturers is direct marketing to possible patients. The idea is to motivate patients to pressure their doctors into prescribing the product. Any baseball fan is likely to have seen flashing ads during televised games for Viagra, a drug used to treat sexual dysfunction in males, or others of its type. The legal departments of pharmaceutical companies engaged in this tactic do at times try to reduce company liability by squeezing a dense disclaimer into the end of the advertisement packed with side effects and the directive to "Ask your doctor."

However, the net psychological result of such aggressive drug marketing is unfortunate. It creates an attitude that drugs are not only meant to treat disease, but to regulate all human functions from cradle to grave. Even if not all joint pain is arthritis, when the supposed benefits of a drug to cure this pain is heralded on a television advertisement, there is a message to people, whose sore joints may come from a day's work in the garden, to pressure their doctors for the drug. If adults are sanctioned to take a pill for every pain, what is the message we give to our children?

Drug Misinformation

In war the first casualty is truth and it is no different during the so-called War on Drugs. Misinformation is not new. Propaganda films mounted against marijuana in the 1930s (*Reefer Madness, Devil's Harvest* and *Marijuana: Weed with Roots in Hell*) served up misinformation in such ludicrous portions that they have become staples for the argument that the government only lies to you about drugs. To this day such bureaus as the National Institute on Drug Abuse and the National Academy of Sciences are tarred with the same brush. However, these old films were produced in an era devoid of scientific data. Today we are drenched in a data downpour. The game then becomes selecting only data that supports your position.

Even as the pendulum swings toward a more sympathetic view of marijuana, drug policy authorities don't seem to get the drug problem right. One recent summary from the Netherlands of the medical possibilities of marijuana, for example, dismisses the connection between intense marijuana use and subsequent heroin and cocaine addiction as affecting "only a tiny fraction of the adult population." That "tiny fraction" turns out to be as high as 800,000 people in the United States today. If increased access to pot leads to increased use, will that lead to millions more heroin and cocaine addicts? Is medicinal marijuana "safe" by this measure? According to some advocates it is, if it is kept in the hands of the physicians. But most of the important data aren't in. So in the meanwhile, what do we tell the kids?

Worse yet, in six states the fight to legalize marijuana for medical purposes has been taken out of the hands of doctors and put into those of politicians. The image of supporters of California Proposition 215 lighting up a celebratory joint the day the Proposition passed appears to have tainted the effort as a disingenuous tactic in the battle for the legalization of marijuana in general, rather than a legitimate claim of medical science for its use for medical purposes. The battle has been waged on the political front and carried on with the political tools of deep pockets, war chests and ad campaigns. By 1998 six states voted to legalize medical marijuana. Claimed Dennis Peron, a drafter of California's Prop 215 and manager of the San Francisco Cannabis Cultivators Club, "All use of marijuana is medical."

Although marijuana has been considered for use in patients with AIDS, glaucoma, multiple sclerosis and other illnesses, a review of the question by the Institute of Medicine in 1999 called for clinical trials of medical marijuana, not clinical use. This is where the claims must be verified. There is a big difference between medical trials and anecdotal evidence. The most recent voice to weigh in on this question is the United States Supreme Court, which, in 2001, concluded in an opinion by Justice Thomas that federal law does not allow a "medical necessity" exception to the prohibition on the distribution of marijuana, but does not overturn state initiatives. Controversy among adults may be good for democracy, but it's difficult to explain to kids. If a child lacks confidence in what adults say about drugs and especially adults in positions of responsibility, the child is likely to turn to other kids for information or as thousands of kids have told me over the years, draw conclusions from their own experiences.

Misinformation also washes over our children from television shows and film. The successful Hollywood offering, *Pulp Fiction*, vividly portrays shooting up, which prompted one non-drug using filmmaker to say, "It was so beautiful it made *me* want to shoot heroin." This is drug abuse prevention in reverse. Less spectacular, but more persistent, are the beer commercials brimming over with macho role models and the gorgeous gals who love them. While the pseudomedicalization of marijuana is an unfortunate tactic, the political effort to legalize the drug in California, Arizona and other states is laudable in one regard. The effect of the so-called War on Drugs has been to make criminals of people whose behaviors in other countries would be judged misdemeanors or personal choices. Reducing or repealing costly, cruel and counterproductive drug laws is both rational and just.

The leading source of drug misinformation is also the most potent technology reaching kids today, the Internet. Individual users have the ability to set up a personal drug-related page and transmit drug recommendations in cyberspace to any kid with a personal computer. Other Internet sites offer to sell drugs or drug producing plants through the mail. The marketing of dangerous drugs through the mail is a public menace. This fact has already begun to dawn on a number of Internet servers providing pro-drug information. One website, devoted to information about the particularly toxic hallucinogenic plant, *Salvia divinorum*, has clearly formulated its message on the advice of legal counsel. In bold type a disclaimer says, "The entire risk as to the quality and/or accuracy of the information on this server is with you."

Be aware that not everything your kid reads about drugs on the Internet is reliable. The remainder of this book won't answer every question you have about drugs, but I'll try to deal with the most significant. Putting an end to this epidemic begins with knowledge for parents.

At the end of each chapter, I put what I think are the most important points. Here is Take-Home Lesson #1.

Take-Home Lesson #1

1) All drugs are dangerous, depending on how they're used and who is using them.
2) Half of our children have used an illicit drug by their senior year in high school.
3) Drug use by kids has reached the epidemic stage.
4) Parents have the responsibility and ability to put an end to this epidemic.

Chapter 2

Kids at Risk:
Do Genes Matter?

The short answer is, yes, genes matter. They are the ties that bind families into generations of illness, a vivid example being the disease of alcoholism. Often I am asked if alcoholism can "skip a generation." Or if a parent has had an addiction in the past, but now is recovered, should she still be worried about her child? What if both parents had addictive histories? Is the risk doubled in their children? And which comes first, the alcoholic behavior or the addictive genes? Do genes always govern behavior or can behavior change genes? Finally, can healthy genes mutate into an alcoholic condition? Research on these questions is moving along rapidly and the results point to powerful connections between one's chemical heritage and one's subsequent vulnerability to drug use.

The general strategy for studies that look to make a connection between genes and a particular illness is to see if that illness is present or absent more consistently in identical twins than in fraternal ones. As you know, a pair of fraternal twins is genetically no different from any other pair of brothers or sisters. That is, while half their genes come from each parent, there is no telling which ones a child will get in the gene shuffle that occurs at fertilization. That means they're similar, but not the same. That's *not* the case with identical twins, who share 100 percent of their genes with each other. This makes for a powerful tool in searching for a genetic basis for any number of conditions, including drug addiction.

If we were to look for a genetic basis for alcoholism, we might assemble a large group of twins, both fraternal and identical and then screen them for alcohol dependence. If identical twins are more often consistent with each other regarding the presence or absence of alcoholism than fraternal twins, the likely explanation is alcohol-vulnerable genes. What's hot is that this type of study has been done a number of times with similar results. The bottom line is this: there appears to be a genetic factor in alcoholism. If you have a brother or sister who is alcoholic, your chances of becoming alcoholic yourself are higher than for folks whose siblings are tee-totalers. If your identical twin is alcoholic, you have an even higher risk—four to twelve times greater than the general public. But—and this is crucial for parents to keep in mind—the probability of developing alcoholism, even if your identical twin is alcoholic, is *not* 100 percent.

As important as this research is, there is a problem with typical twin studies. Most often, twins are raised in the same home. How, then, can you tell if the alcoholic behavior is due to a genetic pre-disposition or if the environment has played a significant role? You can't. But researchers are pretty smart and they've figured a way around this weakness in twin studies. Suppose the child of an alco-holic parent is adopted at birth by non-alcoholic parents. He would not have the drinkers' environment from his biological parents to explain the disease and yet would still carry his biological parents' genes into his new home. If alcoholism has a genetic basis, those genes should bring a greater risk for the disease than the genes of adopted kids whose biological parents were not alcoholic. And that's what's been found in every study, in Denmark, Sweden and the United States. In other words, if a child has an alcoholic bio-logical parent, *even if he or she is raised by non-alcoholic adoptive parents*, the risk of developing the disease is increased.

Certainly the most precise way to answer if alcoholism has a genetic component is to find the gene. A gene is a coded piece of DNA that contains building instructions for protein—what makes us *us*. But of the estimated 100,000 different genes we humans carry around inside our cells, few are identified completely in terms of location and function. Alcoholism, at least if we look at studies in humans, does not seem to be the result of a single gene, but rather multiple genes acting in concert or different genes acting singly in different people to give the same result. To help narrow the hunt, a group of researchers at the Veterans Administration Medical Center in Portland, Oregon, turned to the lowly mouse for an answer.

Given half a chance, a mouse will drink alcohol. Using this knowledge, T.J. Phillips and colleagues in Oregon identified two genetically different types of mice: one that was indifferent to the taste of alcohol and one that we can call the party animal, who thought alcohol tasted just dandy. Then they crossed these two types and examined which of the offspring were big drinkers like the parent party animal. Then they tested which of the thousands of regions of the offsprings' genes correlated with alcohol preference. To date at least twenty-four such needles in the mouse's genetic haystack have been mapped that are associated with alcohol-related behaviors.

This work shows that genes in mice are linked to alcohol preference. Since humans have many of the same genes as mice (adding a new answer to my father's question, "Are you a man or a mouse?") the hunt is on in humans for addiction-related genes as well. What do scientists think these genes do to predispose a person to drink her way to addiction? A number of ideas appear likely:

- Genes may predispose a person to seek alcohol, a trait that has been shown to be the case in a number of other creatures.
- Genes may cause individuals to react differently to alcohol, as anyone who has spent time in the vicinity of a holiday party punch bowl can attest.
- Certain genes may predispose a person to become addicted to alcohol.

At this point you may be wondering why it matters if genes are involved in alcoholism. Simply put, genetic knowledge is therapeutic power. Genes help us predict future illness before it occurs, whether it be heart disease or alcoholism. For those of us at risk, genes may help us devise preventive strategies. And because genes ultimately govern how the body functions, they offer clues for medical interventions in a broad range of diseases, including the addictions.

What We Know So Far about Genes and Alcohol

Earlier in this chapter I spoke of questions that I have heard from worried parents over the years. Now we have good genetic knowledge to answer these questions. Let's take them one at a time.

Worried Parent: Can alcoholism "skip a generation?"

A: Yes, it can. And, thankfully, it can come to a complete halt *despite* a strong genetic history. (More about this in later chapters.)

WP: What if I've had an addiction in the past, but am now recovered? Should I still be worried about my child?

A: Yes, you should. Genes can take over or other factors can keep them under control. Your recovery is almost as important to your child as it is to you. It can serve to reduce your child's risk of a similar addiction.

WP: What if both my spouse and I had addictive histories? Would the risk be increased in our children?

A: Yes, the risk would in all likelihood be increased. The result would be like a one-two punch. These kids should be considered at the highest risk for alcoholism and probably other addictions as well. But once again, your recoveries are crucial to tipping the scales in your child's favor.

WP: Which comes first, the alcoholic behavior and then addictive genes, or is it the other way around?

A: This is the twenty-first century equivalent of the old chicken-and-egg problem. That is, which comes first, the addictive behavior or the troubled genes? The take-home answer according to current thinking is that genes come first and then the environment exerts an influence on what kind of chicken you end up with. With alcoholism, you start off with genes vulnerable to alcohol and the environment tips the scales one way or another.

WP: What about mutations? Can't they lead to genetic problems like alcoholism?

A: It's true that mutations can occur in humans from such things as radiation or viruses and result in rare diseases such as

Huntington's disease and hemophilia. But the human genome is really quite a stable masterwork. Alcoholic genes already appear in such abundance in people that a spontaneous mutation would be hard to detect. We never say never, but the prospect of some mutation producing a spider the size of Cincinnati, a radioactive superhero—or an alcoholic—so far has only occurred in the movies.

WP: What if there is an active alcoholic in the home now?

A: Genes aside, the child is at serious risk for harm on multiple levels. Get help for the parent. Protect the child. In the next two chapters, you will learn what you need to do. Then take action. Yes, I know that treating alcoholism is a tough, long road. All the more reason to get to work on the problem today. This last question brings me to the most powerful forces in combating drugs and alcohol in kids: moms, dads, you. You who are reading this book, feeling worry, doubt and discouragement can be the most powerful force. You can become your kid's hero.

How Moms and Dads Can Make the Difference

You may be wondering, if genes may cause alcoholism, how can it skip generations? And why is it that even identical twins don't always end up with the same alcohol problem? What is missing in this puzzle so far is the piece I've saved for last and the most important piece: the power of a parent. Pierre's story poignantly illustrates this power.

The son of French Canadian parents, Pierre grew up with his mother, Michele and sister, Donna. His parents had separated after Pierre's father's drinking progressed to the point that his mother could no longer bear the longshoreman's misspent paychecks, the late-night calls from emergency rooms and the broken furniture. Michele had only a fifth-grade education, but she was long on common sense. She had known her husband's father and his three brothers. All of them had suffered from alcoholism. Her own father had been a drinker as well and, on some level, she came to realize she had married her husband to rescue her father symbolically. But if she had failed with her husband, she did not want to fail with her son, Pierre.

Beginning when he was a small child, Michele educated her son about his father's illness. She told him she feared it ran in families. She warned him that for others alcohol was social, but for him it would be suicidal. That fact was driven home on the sad occasions when he would see his father sitting on a corner with friends, passing a bottle in a bag until they passed out.

Theirs was a religious family and Pierre did well in the local Catholic school he attended, which reinforced the ideal of sobriety. However, one night when he was a teen he came home drunk, Michele flew into a helpless rage and wept. It was the last time Pierre appeared drunk at home. But he did not remain abstinent.

Each time he drank, he looked at himself and asked if he was turning into his father. His girlfriend left him. The police served him with a citation for driving while intoxicated. He lost his job in an electronics firm for absenteeism. It was hard to show up for work if you started your day with a six-pack. I treated him for his first and last detox, when he was twenty-eight. With pale face, deep circles under his eyes and a six-day's growth of beard, he saw the writing on the wall. He joined Alcoholics Anonymous and attended meetings for a year. At the time of my last appointment with him two years later he had continued to remain sober.

"I knew on one level my mom was right about me and booze. But there was always this little voice in me saying, 'Take the drink. Go for it. You're not really like your dad.' I live with that voice everyday. But now I know it's a liar. It's my mom who was telling the truth."

As the twig is bent, I thought, *so grows the tree.*

While Pierre's genes may have explained his alcohol abuse, it was the concerted effort of his mother and his community that planted the seeds of his recovery. Genes simply don't explain the *whole* story. And in that there is a mountain of hope. Human behaviors and institutions *can* be changed. To me it's tremendously reassuring to know that if you have an alcoholic identical twin, there is a 40 – 70 percent chance you will *not* develop the disease. What can explain this variability? The effects of education, the environment and, most of all, what I call Heads Up Parenting. That's where we fathers and mothers can roll up our sleeves and make a difference. The next chapter tells how.

Take-Home Lesson #2

1) Genes matter in alcoholism and possibly other addictions as well.
2) Vulnerable Genes + Unhealthy Environment = Trouble.
3) Genes are not the whole story. A safe or dangerous environment can be decisive in determining whether a kid turns to drugs and alcohol.
4) Fathers and mothers can and must make a difference.

Chapter 3

Heads-up Parenting:
Red Flags and Golden Halos

"Is my kid at risk for drug abuse?"
"How can I tell?"
"If not, how can it be prevented?"
"If so, how can it be treated?"

These are the most important questions a parent can ask about kids and drugs. The next two chapters try to give you the answers. Given the right (or wrong) set of environmental influences, every kid is at risk for drug abuse. The answer then is to reduce the risk by altering the environment.

We've made a lot of progress in identifying which kids and, more importantly, which risk factors in kids' lives increase the chance of future drug and alcohol use. Think of it as a kind of crystal ball developed by studying hundreds of thousands of kids over the past four decades. Looking into this ball helps us predict which kids are more, or less, likely to get into trouble from drugs and alcohol. Predicting future drug use in kids is important, because preventing drug abuse is a heck of a lot easier than treating it.

Descending the Stairway from Heaven

Jason's father, a hard-driving litigator, had steadily provided his family with a six-figure income. Jason did not want for anything: private school, costly camps, a lovely upscale suburban home. Unfortunately, his learning disorder was not picked up at home or his private school. He was eleven when he took to smoking cigarettes in the tool shed in his spacious backyard. Losing interest in school, he also lost the anxiety of being caught smoking by his parents and began smoking before and after school with his friends.

He enjoyed no team sports, had increasingly poor grades and no apparent interest in after-school activities except skateboarding. His mood at home was sullen, angry and depressed. So when a friend offered him some marijuana as a pick-me-up, his response was "Cool!" Pot soon became a crutch to get through the day. He found that school was becoming a hostile and inexplicable territory, which he dealt with by a cycle of playing hooky and smoking, until he left school permanently at sixteen. His father tried to get him jobs, but he held them erratically, since the trail of marijuana followed him wherever he went.

When the marijuana started to lose its magic, Jason found the idea of heroin intriguing, especially when his friends promised there would be "no needles." At his first snort, he felt nauseated and then mellow for the first time in memory. Over the next few months heroin, became his new best friend. When he didn't have it on hand, withdrawal became his most frightening enemy. One night a drug buddy showed him how to shoot the drug and he told himself the biggest lie an addict can tell himself. He "had to do what he had to do."

In no time, Jason was into his dealer for a several-hundred-dollar-a-week habit. To support it, he began to steal, at first from his family, then his friends and, finally, from neighbors' homes when they were on vacation. When pickings were slim, he graduated to armed robbery. His recovery from addiction only began after he was wounded during an attempted robbery of a pharmacy for Oxycontin, a narcotic pain reliever.

The Gateway Theory

Jason's story exhibits a number of common milestones in the stumble to addiction. Starting with legal drugs (tobacco), users progress to misdemeanor drugs (marijuana) and then to felony drugs (heroin). This is known as "the gateway theory," an important finding of Professors Denise Kandel at Columbia and Gene Smith at Harvard, among others. Thankfully, the majority of kids who take the first step or two do not go farther.

This fact has led to some misunderstanding of what the gateway idea is all about. This hypothesis flags certain behaviors that increase *the risk* of addiction. It does not predict that *all* kids experimenting with legal or misdemeanor drugs will progress inexorably to felony drugs, anymore than skydiving always leads to crash landings.

Let's do some of the numbers. This work is by researchers Andrew Golub and Bruce Johnson and was published in 2001 in the *American Journal of Public Health*. If you track 100,282 people for eighteen years (exhausted yet?) to at least until age twenty-six, you find that roughly 85 percent of them use alcohol or tobacco at some point in their lives. 21.7 percent of the 100,000 proceeded to add marijuana use to the list and 7.7 percent proceeded to add hard drugs. However, these researchers also noted that an increasing number of hard drug users did *not* follow the gateway path, particularly inner city kids.

So where does that leave us with the gateway theory? Marijuana use, especially heavy use, counts as a predictor for moving on to hard stuff, but it is hardly the whole story. What does this say about our public war against marijuana use? Our leaders reasoned that if we stamped out marijuana, following the predictions of the gateway theory, other drug abuse would be stamped out as well. So far, so bad. This policy, which has inspired the spending of literally billions of tax dollars in the War on Drugs, is reminiscent of the drunk who loses his keys at night and insists on looking for them under a lamppost, because that's where the light is. The policy also shifts the responsibility of drug prevention the wrong way, from parents, where it should be, to law enforcement authorities, where it shouldn't. There are *many factors* that lead a kid into hard drugs, not just the softer ones. A lot of the factors happen right under a parent's nose. Some of them are dangers. Others actually protect a kid. Here's what to look for.

What to Watch For: Red Flags and Golden Halos

If we look into our crystal ball, we can find a number of signs in a kid, his family and friends that can foretell his or her future choices about drugs. I call the worrisome signs Red Flags and the healthy ones Golden Halos. At least 384 factors are thought to predict drug use in kids. Not all warning signs are equally strong. In the pioneering longitudinal studies of Denise Kandel, Gene Smith and others in this field, we can see four broad classes of predictors that emerge from the literature:

1) a teen's behaviors, personality traits and values
2) the role of parents
3) the influence of peers
4) preexisting psychiatric illness

Tables 3 through 8 list the most common Red Flags and Golden Haloes that affect a teen's risk of drug abuse. However, a few notes of caution should be sounded. These factors are not definite predictors of any *individual* kid's future and should *not* be used to single out innocent kids before they are proven guilty. Instead, use these tables to identify which behaviors and values to encourage in your child, with the confidence that such an effort is likely to reduce (not absolutely prevent) drug use in the future.

At this point, a few words are needed about the strengths and weaknesses of "predicting" future drug use. The reader will quickly recognize that anyone's ability to predict anything about the future seldom gets high marks for accuracy. And so a certain degree of humility is indicated when we claim to be able to predict which kids are likely to use drugs in the future. We simply cannot know *with certainty* if our concerns will be borne out. The red flags (and golden halos) are based on statistics. They cannot and should not be misused to make judgments about individual kids. Some maturity is needed in using predictors of drug use.

I have not included the nearly four hundred variables that have been studied as possible predictors of drug use, not because they are not important, but because I've chosen the most powerful ones that can make a difference in a family's life. When reflecting on these predictors, think like the Las Vegas odds maker who observed, "The race does not always go to the swift, nor the battle to the strong, but that's the way you place the bets."

Finally, let me make a distinction between drug experimentation, drug abuse and addiction. The first occurs because kids want to know what all this drug and alcohol fuss is about. They want to be like their peers, regress from the adulthood pressures that loom before them or become adventurers of the mind. However, the last two, abuse and addiction, are trouble. If you're worried your kid is involved in any of the three, but you can't tell which, it's time to bring in reinforcements. Usually this means a consult with a psychiatrist, psychologist or social worker with drug counseling experience to decode what's going on.

Risky Business:
What Kids Do to Increase the Chance of Drug Abuse

This one is easy: they smoke cigarettes. Far and away this one behavior predisposes to later use of marijuana and hard stuff. It makes sense. Aside from knowing how to eat a marijuana brownie, you have to know how to smoke to use marijuana. Smoking cigarettes is a gateway to marijuana. It is also the earliest addiction. What follows, not *always,* I must add, is that the gateway effect of marijuana is to stronger stuff like LSD and cocaine. Daily cigarette smokers have a ten-fold increase in risk of using marijuana and cocaine. Other big red flags for future drug use are delinquency, cutting class at school and alcohol use in all three forms—beer, wine and liquor.

An important point regarding the use of gateway drugs (alcohol, marijuana and tobacco) is that the younger a kid starts, the more serious the eventual outcome becomes. For example, a kid who smokes pot before the age of twelve is forty-two times more likely to use cocaine or heroin than a kid who first came to pot after age sixteen.

The negative effects of early use apply to alcohol as well. Avoid giving kids "sips" of alcohol on "special" occasions and discourage alcohol use before your child is of legal age. To do otherwise sends the message that drinking is okay for kids, which it is not. Early use of alcohol in the short run does worse things to kids than it does to adults. Liver enzymes for alcohol in children are absent or immature, which means that along with a smaller body mass, the brain of a child is less protected from alcohol than the brain of an adult. The "cute" picture of a drunken child at the Christmas dinner is a picture of a child with brain toxicity. And since children have erratic judgment to begin with—alcohol only makes their judgment worse. To me, the only thing scarier than a drunk driver is a drunk teenaged driver.

Interestingly, political activity is also a predictor of future drug use, at least as far as future marijuana use is concerned. This last should not be a total surprise, particularly since our last two Presidents had histories of drug use in their youth, even if one swore on a stack of Bibles he didn't inhale. But it doesn't make sense to attempt to restrain a child from political activism, any more than it does to attempt to ban elections of class officers. The point of heads-up parenting is not to suppress democracy (that goes on too much as it is). In all likelihood a child's political activity can signal an independence of mind or rebelliousness of spirit. These are not bad in themselves, even if they can predispose a kid to embark on a drug adventure.

On a positive note, kids who go to church, synagogue or other religious services regularly are at reduced risk for drug use. The major world religions exert social control or outright bans of intoxicants. Religion is not a panacea for the drug problem in kids, but, in my opinion, it's under-appreciated as a constructive force in promoting abstinence. If you have a bit of the religious spark in you, fan it into a flame and support it in your kids. Adolescents are open to asking the Big Questions and challenging them head-on. They are especially inclined to do it with their peers (and less so with their parents). If they want to go to a religion-sponsored youth group, this is your chance to get them to the "church" on time.

If you're an agnostic or atheist, you can and should help your kids develop senses of moral responsibility without religious institutions setting the agenda.

Kids who get good grades also are at reduced risk for using drugs.

On the negative side, poor grades are a clear red flag for drug use. Kids on drugs don't get, or keep, good grades. Sooner or later even high achievers tend to crash and burn. Use your parental radar to pick up early problems in the kid who used to get good grades and now is slipping downwards or the kid who always struggled in school and now has slipping self-esteem. Helping a kid boost his confidence academically and in other ways can reverse a hazardous trend.

Another flag is an erratic performance on standardized tests of math and language skills. Tests that are repeated over time are more valuable in this regard, since a kid who was drug free at one point in the past will test worse later if he is using. If a child tests considerably below her previous level, consider a red flag to be present, all the while remembering that drug use is only one of a dozen possible explanations. For a kid like Jason, who had an attention deficit disorder, the key is rapid discovery and intervention, *before* a career of school failure batters the child into alienation. Otherwise, the kid with this kind of profile faces greater hazards of drug use.

On the left side of Table 3, there is a list of behaviors in which a kid may engage. Some are dangerous. Some are healthy. Across the tip of the Table is a row of future possible drugs of abuse ("Hard Liquor, Marijuana and Other Drugs"). Notice there are a bunch of red flags and golden halos. Each red flag means that a specific behavior *increases* the risk of future use of liquor, dope or other drugs. Each golden halo means that the behavior in its row *reduces* the chance of future use of liquor, dope and other drugs. Let's take a look at a specific behavior, "Smoking cigarettes," for example. In the row for "Smoking cigarettes" is a red flag under "Hard Liquor," "Marijuana" and "Other Drugs." This means that smoking cigarettes increases the risk of each of these drug use activities *in the future*.

Look down the table at the behavior "Good grades." You will see a golden halo under each of the drugs studied. This means that good grades *reduce* the chance a kid will use those drugs in the future. If certain categories don't have a flag or halo, such as between "Prior Drug Dealing" and using "Hard Liquor," it means the research hasn't been done to prove the link. But remember, despite the correlations shown in the table, you must use common sense. A kid who is selling drugs, for example, is in trouble, flag or no flag, with or without a dietary supplement of hard liquor.

**TABLE 3: Personal Behaviors That Affect
a Kid's Risk for Future Drug**

Kids Behaviors	That Influence Starting:		
	Hard Liquor	Marijuana	Other Drugs
Smokes cigarettes	⚑	⚑	⚑
Use of beer and wine	⚑	⚑	⚑
Prior use of marijuana		⚑	⚑
Uses marijuana for self understanding		⚑	⚑
Prior drug dealing		⚑	⚑
Major delinquent behavior			⚑
Cuts classes	⚑	⚑	
Minor delinquent behavior	⚑	⚑	
Good grades	◯	◯	◯
Attends church regularly	◯	◯	◯

Stinkin' Thinkin':
Kids' Values That Stack the Odds against Them

Kids are value magnets. They pick up values wherever they find them. First and foremost they get them from their parents. It may be hard to believe that your adolescent even hears 5 percent of what you tell him, but kids at that age struggle against what you know with what he thinks is better. From the Department of Easy Advice (easy to say, hard to do): Shrink not from the fray! You're supposed to wave your arms, sharpen your tongue and raise the heat in the living room with animated discourse.

Certain *values* your kids hold today predict potential drug and alcohol use tomorrow. High on the worry list are positive attitudes towards alcohol and marijuana. A teen who talks a great deal about marijuana, supports its legalization and endorses its alleged virtues, is sending an unmistakable message that smoking dope is a near-term possibility.

On the other hand, when a teen expresses knowledge of the harm of using drugs or alcohol, he inoculates himself against future dangers. Like any other vaccine, it may not work 100 percent of the time, but it helps. Ironically, a value that we ordinarily encourage in kids—independent thinking—can get a kid in trouble with drugs. Kids do better, though, when they see their parents as concerned about drug use and when they themselves value doing well in school. A kid who values school performance gets points, too, even if his grades don't reflect it. But then weak grades are a red flag that says he could use a bit of extra help in that department.

So how does a parent counteract the negative values that lead to drug or alcohol use? To begin, dispense with the don't-ask-don't-tell principle from the Army. *Do* ask and *do* tell. *Ask* your child what he thinks about marijuana. *Tell* him your views. The openness such a discussion can bring about will be refreshing. Needless to say, your words as parents will not be half so influential on your children as your actions. There is little point in telling your child not to drink if she sees one or more parents under the influence of alcohol on a regular basis.

Now let's look at Table 4. It summarizes which values in kids predict future use of hard liquor, marijuana or other drugs. A kid who values both marijuana and smoking cigarettes is more likely to end up smoking pot. No surprise. But it's important to recognize the power of the opposite values. That is, a kid who sees the use of pot or smoking as harmful is *less* likely to use drugs in the future.

As in Table 3, the presence of a flag or halo in Table 4 means that the association has been nailed down well by research studies. An absence of a flag or halo again means that the research hasn't been definitive or hasn't been done. Again, don't see this as an invitation for your common sense to take a vacation. A kid who lusts after dope is most likely at risk for alcohol and other drugs as well. Similarly, when a kid values scholastic achievement, even if she's not an honor student, such a value may exert a positive effect in the future on her ability to resist using marijuana or other drugs.

TABLE 4: Kids' Values Influencing a Risk for Future Drug Use

Kids Values	That Influence Starting:		
	Hard Liquor	Marijuana	Other Drugs
Expresses pleasure from liquor	🚩	🚩	
Desire to use marijuana		🚩	
Thinks marijuana should be legalized		🚩	
Values independence		🚩	

Positive attitudes about
    smoking

Negative attitudes about
    smoking

Sees casual liquor as
    harmful

No desire to experience
    marijuana

Sees regular marijuana
    as harmful

Sees casual heroin as
    harmful

Parents seen as
    discouraging pot

Values scholastic achievement

The Power of Personality

It's a good bet that personality traits come from inborn, genetic programs, which then are modified by experience. But personality traits, regardless of origin, can signal future promise and worries for a mom or dad who practices heads-up parenting skills. The good news is that there are many more traits that work to protect a kid than hurt him. Thus, kids who see themselves and are seen, as hardworking, competent, responsible and self-reliant are less likely to be

messing around with drugs than kids who are impulsive or rebel-
lious. Table 5 will help you: 1) identify which way a kid is heading
and 2) which traits you should support to help healthy growth.

**TABLE 5: Personality Traits Influencing
a Kid's Risk for Future Drug Use**

Kids Personality Traits	That Influence Starting:		
	Hard Liquor	Marijuana	Other Drugs
Rebellious	🚩	🚩	🚩
Impulsive	🚩	🚩	🚩
Trustworthy	🥇	🥇	🥇
Hardworking	🥇	🥇	🥇
Competent	🥇	🥇	🥇
Responsible		🥇	
Ambitious	🥇	🥇	🥇
Self-reliant	🥇	🥇	🥇
Orderly	🥇	🥇	🥇
Feels accepted	🥇	🥇	🥇

The Road to Double Trouble: Psychiatric Disorders

Recent research shows that a child with depressive symptoms may turn to alcohol or street drugs as a form of self-medication. Alcohol or cocaine make excellent antidepressants, at least for the first twenty minutes. A suffering young person is not likely to turn down a short spell of relief if the suffering is deep enough and the desperation great enough. My guess is that the most commonly used anti-depressant in America is marijuana, for a number of reasons. It's available without a doctor's prescription. It's relatively cheap. A month's supply can be had more cheaply than a month's supply of a typical SSRI antidepressant. Marijuana works right away, compared to the two to four-week wait for conventional medication to be effective. And pot carries with it a certain amount of prestige for adolescents, connoting risk, rebelliousness and independence of mind. The fact that, unlike legal drugs it has not been proven to work as a long-term antidepressant is not likely to be foremost in the mind of a depressed teenaged doper.

In addition to depression, other psychiatric disorders are linked to increased drug consumption, including conduct disorder, schizophrenia, post-traumatic stress disorder and anxiety problems. The fact that twenty-five percent of kids with attention deficit hyperactivity disorder (ADHD) also develop conduct disorder may explain why the former has been thought, probably erroneously, to be a risk factor for future drug use. Let me say a few words about conduct disorder. This is clearly a red flag for future drug use, but it is much more than that. Kids with conduct disorder should be viewed as red-flag children, needing a range of social services beyond treatment for drug abuse. Consider the story of Michael.

Born into a chaotic home, he had four siblings and his mother was a prostitute. When he was ten, he was arrested with a group of boys who set fire to a local abandoned factory building. At twelve, he was caught dropping bricks from a bridge onto rowers passing on the river below him. At the time of the arrest for this offense, it was not known that he was also running drugs for a local cocaine dealer. At fourteen, he had his first sexual experience, the rape of a younger sister. By the age of sixteen, following several months in juvenile detention for street robberies, he was experienced with alcohol, cocaine and heroin.

Clearly, Michael's appalling life path was a chain of disasters, not simply the early use of drugs, the causes of which were societal failures at multiple points. But drug use certainly amplified those failures and helped to solidify them in locking Michael and society, into a no-win condition. His case illustrates common features of conduct disorder: aggression, cruelty, forced sex, destruction of property, theft and a blindness to society's rules.

The kid with a psychiatric problem who chooses drugs does not often do so with his or her psychiatric disorder diagnosed. More often self-medication occurs in the face of *undiscovered* psychiatric problems, which means that kids moving into the drug scene should have careful diagnostic assessments. Table 6 lists the psychiatric disorders associated with hard liquor, marijuana and other types of drugs.

**TABLE 6: Psychiatric Disorders Influencing
a Kid's Risk for Future Drug Use**

Psychiatric Disorders	That Influence a Kid Starting:		
	Hard Liquor	Marijuana	Other Drugs
Conduct Disorder	▰	▰	▰
Post-Traumatic Stress Disorder	▰	▰	▰
Anxiety disorders	▰		▰
Mood disorders and depression	▰		▰
Schizophrenia			▰

For Better and Worse:
What the Family Does to Change the Odds of Drug Use

Another huge influence on a youngster's choice to use drugs comes from her parents' words and, more importantly, behavior. The power of an adult serving as a model for a child is great, either by imitation or the complete opposite. The child who is exposed to a parent's war stories about his or her drug use in the good old days or to a parent's drunkenness or self medication with mind-altering prescription drugs gets a different message about drug use than kids whose parents do not tell such seamy tales. Parents who smoke teach their kids to smoke, whether they want to or not. And smoking is the most utilized road to other drugs. A parent's use of a drug increases a biological child's chances for use of the same drug ten times.

Poor family management skills can play a major role in future drug use, as can separations, divorce and physical and sexual abuse. When neither parent is actively involved, either because of career or economic pressures, his or her children's risk of using drugs rise. Prison time for a parent puts a child at risk. A father's drug use or his absence is an especially strong risk factor for a kid's drug use. A teen left to his own devices in the face of decreased input from a parent is a problem. Thus, one of the ironies of the War on Drugs is that imprisoning a drug addict parent increases the likelihood that his or her children will also turn to drugs.

Are you under the impression that blue collar or inner city social class is a big risk for drugs? Wrong! A study by Suniya Luthar and her colleagues at Columbia University found that affluent suburban kids were *more* likely to use illicit drugs than their inner city counterparts. Roughly one out of every three sophomore suburban girls used some kind of illicit drug in the study year, compared to half that rate among inner city girls. This is a national trend, with suburban white kids using more drugs than inner-city African-American and Latino kids. Luthar feels the suburban kids suffer from more academic stress and live in a family and peer culture where it's okay to self-medicate with drugs.

A parent's attitude about drug harm is more effective, according to another recent study, in reducing risk of future drug use than a parent's attempts at strict limit setting. This may be due to the possibility that a teen is inclined to internalize some of his parents' views, make them his own and take them with him wherever he goes. Whereas a teen simply subjected to stiff rules may be inclined to ignore them when a parent is not around to enforce them.

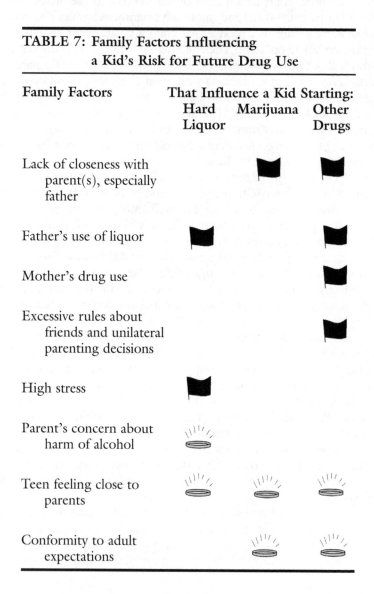

**TABLE 7: Family Factors Influencing
             a Kid's Risk for Future Drug Use**

Family Factors	That Influence a Kid Starting:		
	Hard Liquor	Marijuana	Other Drugs
Lack of closeness with parent(s), especially father		🚩	🚩
Father's use of liquor	🚩		🚩
Mother's drug use			🚩
Excessive rules about friends and unilateral parenting decisions			🚩
High stress	🚩		
Parent's concern about harm of alcohol	😇		
Teen feeling close to parents	😇	😇	😇
Conformity to adult expectations		😇	😇

The Role of Friends

Peer pressure has long been recognized as a risk factor for future drug use. Drugs are commonly used as social glue to bond groups together, dissolve anxiety and provide a common platform for sharing or avoiding experiences. Kids and addicts, call this "partying." One example is the story of Don.

Don began his partying career in high school. Beer was his crowd's drug of choice. Other drugs were not an option for the most part. The time was on weekends, the place was in his parents' spacious finished basement when they were out to dinner or away for weekends. College was an extension of the high school partying. Don wore a tee-shirt with the logo "Born to Party" and a beer company's logo on the front. When he was rushed by three fraternities on campus, he chose the "animal house." For the remainder of his college career, he was drunk or recovering from alcohol almost as many days as he had classes. With family help, he got a job after graduation driving from hospital to hospital selling medical instruments. At twenty-four he was arrested for driving while intoxicated. But contrary to common sense, Don's partying continued, straight through a divorce, two auto accidents, unemployment and a perforated peptic ulcer. When I first met him in the hospital, he told me he got his start as and alcoholic while still a teenager prone to partying.

Don's story of alcoholic partying is typical. It has never ceased to amaze me when I hear an addict describing his downward path to physical, social and economic ruin as partying. Sadly, the use of the word is more than a euphemism. It's also a nostalgic evocation of happier times, even as it leads to so much pain.

In Don's case high school friends and college fraternity brothers influenced him in several ways. They taught him to use alcohol as a social lubricant and legitimized it. That is why it's important to take a good look at your child's friends *now*. Don't wait until he's in college. Try to get to know them while your child lives at home. Table 8 lists the red flags and halos you should look for in your child's friends.

TABLE 8: The Role of Friends in a Kid's Future Choices about Drugs

Factors in Friends	That Influence a Kid Starting:		
	Hard Liquor	Marijuana	Other Drugs
Friends using alcohol or drugs	🚩	🚩	🚩
Abundant conversation about drugs		🚩	🚩
Friends have drugs available			🚩
Lack of intimacy with best friend			🚩
High school age friends	🚩	🚩	
Perception that friends use alcohol	🚩	🚩	
Abundant socializing	🚩	🚩	
Friends approve of drug use		🚩	
Has been offered marijuana or drugs		🚩	
Best friends' concerns about harm from alcohol or drugs	(halo)	(halo)	(halo)

You Are a Big Part of the Environment

Be aware that the likelihood a child will use drugs depends on an interplay between the genes she is born with and what her experiences are in the environment. However, attitudes are not chiseled into genetic stones at conception. Behaviors can be changed. *Parents and peers act as models for healthy attitudes and behaviors.* That's more than half the battle in keeping a child safe. It comes down to this. The risk of future drug use depends on who a child is and what he chooses to do about it. We can't change our genes. For the most part, we can't change how we look or how our brains react to different chemicals. However, we can change our environment by the choices we make for ourselves and our children. You aren't exactly what you eat, but a diet of wholesome foods will have a better effect on you than one of burgers and fries. You are unlikely to develop alcoholism if you live on a desert island without a brewery, no matter what kind of genes you are born with.

It is possible that the interplay between genes and environment is illustrated when specific ethnic groups are studied. Ethnicity may affect drug risks in either direction, depending on the interplay of genetic and environmental factors. Anthropologist Dr. Joan Weibel-Orlando and colleagues at the University of Southern California found in 1984 that Native Americans, for example, have been found to have high rates of alcohol dependence, but the problem was three times as great if Indians in California moved from rural tribal areas to cities. In a similar ethnicity-environment study, epidemiologists R.M. Crum and J.C. Anthony at Johns Hopkins University in 2000 found that African-Americans who dropped out of high school increased the risk for alcohol disorders fourfold, the same as that for whites who dropped out of school.

To drive this last point home, consider an actual study of gene-environment interactions which Dr. G.A. Madrid and colleagues at the Loma Linda University performed in 2001. They found that Latino men who carried an alcoholism gene increased their drinking even more when they were under environmental stress. In dealing with drugs, the environment plays a crucial role. Now let's turn to the best treatment for drug abuse, the heart of heads-up parenting.

Take-Home Lesson #3

1) Smoking cigarettes is one of the strongest predictors of future drug use.
2) Heads-up parents who fight the battle over smoking now reap dividends later.
3) Kids model behavior and attitudes from their family and friends.
4) Heads-up parents are careful of their own drug use.
5) Heads-up parents watch how their kid's friends are behaving.
6) The most powerful force in combating vulnerability to alcohol and drugs is an active, involved mom or dad.

Chapter 4

Prevention:
The Best Treatment

The best treatment for your child is prevention of drug use: not only as a general rule, but specifically because of the biology of addiction. That's because once addiction happens, it's very, very difficult to reverse it. The deeper the drug use, the harder the patterns are to unlearn. In the learning curve, a kid moves from use to abuse and finally from abuse to addiction, the last stop on the drug train. A serious and protracted commitment can make the train go back to its original destination, but a lot of it is uphill. A prevention strategy, by comparison, points a kid in a safer direction from the start.

There is also enormous economic sense in prevention, when you consider that, according to the National Institute of Drug Abuse, the United States is spending $133 billion in 2004 to just pay for the medical complications of addiction. To put that in perspective, $133 billion is exactly one third of what President Bush asked for the entire Department of Defense in 2004. So prevention makes sense, but it has to start at home. As Antonio Maria Costa, the Executive Director of the United Nations Office on Drugs and Crime, figured it in a 2004 speech, "Every dollar invested in treatment and prevention saves *a multiple* — $7 to $10 — for drug-related crime and health costs." He added, "...drug prevention needs to involve society at large...above all, family." Here's a way to think about it.

This strategy can be broken into the Six P's of Prevention. The Six P's of preventing drug abuse in kids are 1) **Person** 2) **Parents**, 3) **Peers**, 4) **Programs**, 5) **Power of the Press** and 6) **Public Policy**. The previous chapter addressed predictors of future drug use which have been gleaned from first-rate studies. Now I want to talk about how Heads-up parents can use them.

Personal Predictors

The First P, Person, refers to *Personal Predictors* of drug use, which are those factors in Tables 3 through 6 of chapter 3. There I've listed red flags and golden halos that point a kid one way or the other. It's important to realize that a mom or dad has a less than perfect ability to affect these factors. As a kid passes through adolescence, a parent's control over his child gets less and less. Control over a teenager is like holding a handful of sand. The longer you do, the less you have. This is healthy, by the way, since a kid learning how to go on dates, drive a car and in general direct her own life, is taking important steps along the path to maturity.

However, when they are teenagers, kids are not mature yet and so control you must, or at least try. The most headway can be made by riding herd on the kid's negative behaviors outlined in Table 3, Personal Behaviors. Making the effort pays a benefit. Putting a veto on smoking of cigarettes and the use of beer or wine cuts down on the probability of future use of marijuana or hard drugs. Even *losing* the battle for cigarettes increases the chance of winning the battle against harder stuff later. The point is: a parent should always fight the battle against cigarettes and alcohol. The same is true with school performance. Encouraging a child to work hard in school and seek positive reinforcers there, benefits her on multiple levels, not the least of which is a reduced chance for future drug use. But you can start even before drugs are an issue. Dr. Robert Zucker and his team at the University of Michigan in 2004 made the remarkable discovery that kids who develop sound sleeping habits as babies *are less likely to abuse drugs as teenagers.*

Tougher to alter is a child's beliefs and values. But that's what effective parenting is about, at least some of the time. What makes the job especially hard is that a child's value system is a moving target. Predictive beliefs and values (listed in Table 4) are among parents' most common battlefields with their adolescents. Some beliefs will be easier to instill than others. A mom who convinces her child that she is adamantly opposed to marijuana use will increase a child's chances of not getting mixed up with pot. Other attitudes in a teen may be harder to change. Common risky attitudes in kids can be heard as calls to battle. Think of them instead as invitations to discourse. "Why shouldn't pot be legalized?" "What's the point of grubbing for grades?" "Don't you want me to think for myself?" "Why can't I drink for fun if I don't get drunk?" When these comments come up (if you are fortunate enough to have a relationship with your son or daughter where these ideas *can* come up), be ready to take them on. To duck the invitation is to ask for trouble by conceding the field to children. Your silence will be read as indifference or even assent.

Wait. It gets harder. Try changing a child's personality. Probably a lot of what we think of as personality is the result of hardwired genetic code, but *not all*. Education counts, example counts, experience counts! Use them all. Don't fall into the trap of saying, "Oh, he's just like his (alcoholic) father," with the implication that nothing helped Dad and so nothing can change junior. Resist the temptation of defeatism. Remember, the earlier you start with a kid, the better the result.

A teen is like a young tree, bent into the shape that you see. Changing the shape of behaviors and beliefs is still possible, but tough and tougher still the longer the task is put off. Can a sloppy child be made into an orderly one? Tough. How about changing a passive child into an ambitious one? Tougher still. Old fashioned Skinnerian conditioning can help some. Skinner pioneered operational conditioning in pigeons and then people, to get them to do complex behaviors. The heart of Skinner's approach is rewards at random intervals for desired behavior. It's important to note punishment is less effective in shaping behavior.

For a child to integrate "hardworking" as a personality trait, he needs to have not only the chance to work, but to reap rewards from the effort. That's where employers, teachers and, most importantly, parents come into the picture. Over years of effort, a child can learn to value hard work. What about the child who doesn't have the ability to take pleasure in anything he does? How can you reward such a child? This is where Dr. Skinner's model falls down and when many parents throw up their hands in despair. This brings us to the next set of predictors of drug use: psychiatric disorders. The first question one should ask about the child who gets pleasure from nothing is whether he is suffering from depression. Marybeth, the subject of the following story, illustrates the problem and the solution.

Marybeth at fourteen appeared to be on a roll. She made the freshman field hockey team, was a B student and loved her art class. Her homework was handed in on time. She earned money baby-sitting, had a new circle of girlfriends from the hockey team and seldom crossed swords with her parents. But by the winter of her freshman year, following the end of the hockey season, her schoolwork began to slip. She got her first failing grade ever at the end of the first semester. The telephone began to ring less often. Marybeth began declining offers of baby-sitting jobs. Her artwork became darker, haunted and sparse. Her two busy parents hoped against hope she would "snap out of it," but when a drawing she had made in school included the word "suicide," an alert art teacher intervened. At my first meeting with Marybeth and her family in my office, I discovered that the child's father and paternal grandmother had been treated for depressions in the past. I treated Marybeth with a course of an antidepressant and psychotherapy on a weekly basis. Eventually, her symptoms of depression were relieved. The following spring one of her paintings was selected for a student competition. The picture showed a small girl, a red house and an overarching tree, all drenched in sunlight.

This fourth class of predictors, psychiatric disorders, as Marybeth's story illustrates, often requires expert help beyond the abilities of the parent. If, like Marybeth, your child exhibits symptoms of serious disturbance, do not feel your child is beyond help. Each of the common precursors to drug abuse — conduct disorder, post-traumatic stress disorder, anxiety and mood disorders and schizophrenia — has a helpful treatment. The key is to get a proper diagnosis before any treatment is undertaken. In an age when physicians have access to a range of powerful psychopharmacological agents and far fewer have training in identification of specific psychiatric entities, the empirical use of medications for non-specific and even vague mental or behavioral conditions is more common than we might wish.

That brings us to the Second P of Prevention.

Parents

You can make the biggest impact on the path your child ultimately takes regarding drug and alcohol use. Parents have a choice here. They can take a passive role and as one mother told me, "sit back and watch them grow." Or they can take an active role in helping a child develop in a healthy direction. The sit-back-and-watch-them-grow philosophy I call Say-wha?- Parenting. Say-wha parents are always surprised when they get calls from the school, police headquarters or the emergency room at night, because it's usually those sources in the community that know first when a kid is in trouble, not the parents. This is the opposite of Heads-up Parenting.

Heads-up parents know when their kid has a dress rehearsal, big test or soccer match. They know the names, addresses and phone numbers of their child's friends. They know where their kid is during the day and night. The list is only partial. The idea is straightforward. Heads-up parents make sure they are informed in what their kids are doing, thinking, valuing and suffering. It's a big job. Nobody does it perfectly. But just making the effort can make a difference.

Heads-up parents give a kid growing competencies in life skills; positive reinforcement for healthy activities in the community; corrective emotional experiences for the tough times kids inevitably go through; a chance to develop altruism and realize that other people have needs, too; a chance to develop long lived relationships with healthy peers; and a chance to establish ties to community centers with the solid values of religious affiliation, team, club and creative ensemble.

Perhaps the most essential value in parent-based prevention is the presence of healthy parents in the first place. Healthy parents take care of themselves. They live their lives as good role models, especially regarding the use of alcohol and drugs. Heads-up Parenting does not require you to abstain from alcohol. There is no danger in the moderate use of alcohol under safe circumstances by healthy adults. Flags start popping up, though, when you begin trying to change any of those basic rules. And it's plain nuts to use alcohol if you've ever had a problem with it in the past.

Heads-up Parents also take the steps needed for a teen ultimately to feel close to them — a tall order during a time of separation and individuation. Jennifer, one girl I met, was a finalist in a state science fair. She had done a creative psychological experiment in which all participants were required to be ignorant of the experimenter's hypothesis. I asked her if every participant in the experiment was kept in the dark about the experiment's purpose. "Oh, yes!" she declared wholeheartedly, "Everyone except my mother."

"Why did you tell her?" I asked.

"Oh," she said, "I tell my mother everything!"

Intact families may be a plus here, but take note of the words "may be." As Tolstoy observed, all happy families are happy in the same way, but not all intact families are happy. Adults who are together can show a kid dangerous drug-related behaviors as well as a single parent can. Divorces can occur for healthy reasons. However, if you are a single parent, there can be twice as much to do, assuming your divorced partner did half of the parenting and is not in the picture now. But Sharlene Wolchik and her team at Arizona State University did a study that should help you take heart in the job ahead. They found that divorced mothers and kids who entered a program of education and support were able to *reduce* the kids' chances of using marijuana, alcohol and other drugs in the future. More Heads-up parenting!

Peers

Remember, as I mentioned earlier, knowing your child's friends is more than friendliness. It is the first line of defense against influence by a kid's friends' dangerous behaviors and attitudes. Knowledge is safety. The obvious flag is the friend with no name, often accompanied by the equally enigmatic answer to where your child's been for the last four hours ("Out."). "Out" or "Nuthin' " should not suffice as answers to inquiries. I am not suggesting a parent establish a local branch of the Federal Bureau of Investigation in the living room. A list of friends, their last names, addresses and home telephone numbers is required. The ideal situation is one of trust between parent and child. But trust is the product of years of truth-telling and increasingly responsible behavior. Trust does not ensure perfect behavior.

With your kid's friends be thoughtful and try to anticipate how kids can get into trouble. That's Heads-up parenting. We can't and shouldn't try to pick our kid's friends. But you shouldn't ignore them either. Don't be in the situation of knowing only the nickname of your youngster's friends.

Adolescence is an intense period of kids coming together and breaking apart. It is also a time in which lasting patterns of friendships develop, which affect the values and goals your kid will carry into adulthood. You will know your child's friends better if you invite them into your home. Tread the line between respecting their need to be alone with each other and setting limits on what will be tolerated on the premises. I always find talking to teenagers exhilarating. Ideas are refreshing even when they are unrestrained by fact. Talking to them about drugs and alcohol does not automatically turn them off drugs, but it is a good first step. Taking a kid home if he shows up at your door drunk shows caring and responsible behavior other kids can emulate. Teaching your child that you will pick him up anywhere, any time and in any condition, is a major confidence builder and may help him avoid a bad situation which could become worse.

Community Programs

The fourth P stands for Programs. A large part of drug abuse prevention can take place at the level of one's community. In the frenzy to "do something" about the drug problem, millions of dollars have been invested in programs aimed at educating kids to keep away from drugs and alcohol. School bulletin boards are dotted with government printed flyers on the topic. School health classes address the issue at younger and younger grade levels. New research is now emerging giving us guideposts about which programs of drug education appear to work and which do not.

What works? The pioneering program, Life Skills Training, by Dr. Gilbert Botvin and his colleagues at Cornell, is a very effective one. Two decades ago Botvin and others hypothesized that psychosocial education aimed at enhancing self-esteem and social skills would help eighth, ninth and tenth graders resist the temptation to experiment with smoking. Starting with 281 kids, this research team reduced the number of new smokers among the kids receiving the educational package, compared to kids who did not. Botvin and his team had based their Life Skills package on intuitively sensible goals—role modeling, reinforcement of desired behaviors, setting normal expectations and teaching kids how to cope with social pressure. Drug education was included. Since then, this educational approach has been refined and validated multiple times. For example, fifteen sessions of Life Skills Training were given to 1,278 girls in seventh grade in New York City compared to a control group of 931 who received no training, with reduction in experimental smoking at one year among the trained girls. In another study, 3,597 students were followed for six years after random assignment to treated or control groups in the sixth grade. The treated kids reported less illicit drug use, with 44 percent fewer drug users and 66 percent fewer polydrug users. Notice the magic words "random assignment." This prospective study ensured that there was no bias in the selection of the groups by randomly assigning the students to either the control group or the treated group, a major plus in credibility.

There are limits to the effectiveness of such programs, however. Once kids have started on drugs, for example, programs such as this one are not effective in getting them to stop. And while kids who are good students are able to make use of drug and life skill education, such programs do not easily address the kids with special needs, that is, the very kids who, as we have seen, are at higher risk for later drug use.

Be aware that not all general drug education programs are equally successful. Consider the track record of the D.A.R.E. program. Created in Los Angeles in 1983 through the cooperation of the Los Angeles police and education departments, D.A.R.E. achieved a meteoric path across the sky of drug education. D.A.R.E., which stands for Drug Abuse Resistance Education, comprises lectures given to primary school and junior high kids by police officers with eighty hours of training in the field of drug education. Growth of the D.A.R.E. program has been impressive: there are now over 7,500 courses being taught on four continents, Australia and New Zealand. But does D.A.R.E. succeed? Sad to say, it doesn't seem to work. Let's look at one of any number of research studies of the D.A.R.E. experience.

In 1999 Donald Lynam and colleagues at the University of Kentucky studied 1,002 kids, some of whom received the D.A.R.E. program and some of whom did not. Kids were tested in elementary school, before the D.A.R.E. program and followed over time to the age of twenty. Did D.A.R.E. reduce drug use? Not according to Lynam's team. At ten years after administration of the D.A.R.E. curriculum, there were no real differences between the kids who took it and the kids who didn't. This is a solid study, but there is no insurance against bias in the results. For example, not every kid returned the questionnaire sent out when he reached the age of twenty. Which kid was more likely to return a questionnaire in the mail? Responsible, compliant and motivated kids. Who gets studied and how they are chosen are important sources of bias. In the Kentucky group's defense, it should be noted that they did attempt to address this problem of attrition in the sample by comparing data gathered at the start of the study between kids who answered their mail at age twenty and those who didn't. Only a small degree of difference was found between the groups, but it's telling that one of the variables that set the two groups apart was that more of the non-responders had been smoking cigarettes in the sixth grade.

This study is better than most and justifiably got much attention in the press when it was first published. The authors tackled the question of why D.A.R.E. has continued to thrive in the absence of proof that it actually works. The first is that it is a feel-good program. It makes intuitive sense to people and helps them feel they're doing something useful about the drug problem. Perhaps more importantly is that if the long term risk of alcohol and drug dependence is low to begin with, then D.A.R.E. may be taking credit when it isn't due. For example, at any given time only 3 percent of the country suffers from alcohol dependence. For young adults between eighteen and twenty-five, only 1 percent used cocaine in the preceding year. That means that 99 percent of that group did not. It's easy to claim success when the natural outcome data are strongly in your favor at the beginning. It would be analogous to giving a kid a 99 on the math test before she took it.

Another little addressed question is whether a police-based drug education program is an asset or liability. We know that parents' strenuous efforts to control kids regarding drugs are not likely to be as effective as healthy parental attitudes about drugs. Whether the perceptions of the police as authority figures overshadows their message is not clear. It should be added that other programs aimed at preventing drug use in kids do not appear to be any more successful. These include programs of emotional education without drug information and alternatives to drugs such as after school sports activities and wilderness programs in pursuit of a "natural high." The general idea of a natural high is a good one. Strenuous aerobic activity releases beta-endorphin, a naturally occurring opioid molecule, from within the body, as any long distance runner will tell you. These create a sense of peace and even a bit of euphoria. Such workouts are the stuff of high school and beyond, not before and high school is also a time of increasing drug experimentation. The result is the sad, frequent spectacle of the athlete who gets on a collision course with drugs and ends his sports career in a chemical haze.

Jonathan Caulkins and his group at RAND's Drug Policy Research Center weighed in on the issue of school-based drug education in 2002. Their analyses concluded that good programs more than paid back the money invested in them in hard money. That is, for every $150 invested in a student the payback was $850. Also of note in this important study is that the greatest sources of benefits came from reduction in the use of the legal drugs, alcohol and tobacco, not the others.

Power of the Press

The media, unfortunately, too often give us prevention in reverse. Drugs and alcohol are popularized in the media in the continuous stream of words and images. But the media should be recognized as two-edged swords—soft, intentional marketers of gateway drugs to the young, but also portrayers of the problems as well. Hollywood has from time to time been able to take a hard look at drugs and alcohol. Sandra Bullock's film, *28 Days*, is as well observed a portrait of addiction and recovery as any, despite a rehab center apparently set in Shangri-La.

In a weird way, Hollywood can be seen as a democracy, where the voters are the customers and every ticket purchased is a vote for more of the similar, if not of the same. Thus, movie audiences choose stars, directors, genres and technologies. At the box office buying a ticket for a film that exalts drug use and killing is your vote for more of the same in the future.

Beyond the power of the ticket booth, there is a more active approach that is noteworthy. In 1979 Cindi Lamb, a Maryland mother, and her five-month-old daughter were struck by a repeat offender drunk driver. Badly hurt, her baby was left with quadriplegia. The following year Lamb mobilized her friends, neighbors and sister victims to co-found Mothers Against Drunk Drivers. Today MADD has over 600 local chapters in the country. Its mission is to "stop drunk driving, support victims of this violent crime and prevent underage drinking."

MADD has made good use of the media. In 1983 NBC produced a film based on the experiences of Candace Lightner, a co-founder of MADD, who had lost a thirteen-year-old daughter to a drunk driver. Following the airing of the film, the number of MADD's chapters grew from about seventy to more than one hundred and ninety. Today there are chapters in every state along with international affiliates. Because of the activities of MADD mothers, over 2,300 alcohol-related laws have been passed in the country, resulting in older ages when drinking legally can start, public education about drinking and driving and stiffer penalties for drunk drivers to back up their words. In the same period of time, alcohol-related traffic deaths in the United States have fallen by over 40 percent. MADD deserves much of the credit. The mothers of MADD are making a difference through political action. This is an excellent example of the link between health and political action. The effectiveness of MADD in large part comes from the strength of its sharply focused message and the development of grassroots activists to improve the nation's laws. This brings us to the last P of Prevention, the setting of national policy.

Influencing Public Policy

In World War II, the German armies quickly overran France. In addition to commandeering the factories, roads, rivers and airports, the Nazis captured the French wine districts. The war itself resulted in falling wine production, which, along with the increased consumption by France's temporary conquerors, resulted in far less wine available for the average Frenchman. As the wine disappeared from the tables of the French, the national prevalence of cirrhosis fell as well. But when the war ended, French wine returned to the tables of the French and the prevalence of cirrhosis in France rose to its pre-war level.

One important lesson from this historic experience is that public restriction of access to alcohol and, by extension, drugs, reduces use and adverse consequences. That's the logic behind raising the minimum age for drinking and raising the price of alcohol. Raising either one reduces consumption. An inventory of possible steps to reduce drug use and its consequences is presented in this book's final chapter. But how is a parent to make any difference whatsoever on the level of national policy?

Several answers come to mind. The first is the injunction of the late Congressman and Speaker of the House Tip O'Neill, who intoned, "All politics is local." By that he meant that people come together in their neighborhoods about matters of common interest. Drug abuse is the ultimate backyard issue, cutting across home, school, workplace, roadways and airways. Although it is also an international issue and as such can demoralize the most ardent parent seeking to effect drug use in her community, drug abuse can be attacked on both ends of the cycle, from producer to user.

The second answer we touched upon earlier: the model of MADD. Besides being media savvy, MADD has clear goals, local emphasis and legislative focus. It would seem to be a given that angry mothers standing up in a state legislature arguing for a higher drinking age would have little opposition. That's not so, however. Who is willing to stand up for more drunks on the highway? The liquor lobby, for one, and elected officials whose campaigns benefit from the largesse of liquor and tobacco lobbies. These are examples of governance by the highest bidder. The MADD model counters that. It's effective, but it's not easy. It requires hard work.

Take-Home Lesson #4

1) Preventing drug abuse is better and more effective than treating it.
2) To prevent it, utilize the 6 P's: Person, Parents, Peers, Programs, Press and Public Policy.
3) The politics of preventing drug abuse should begin in your backyard.
4) Clear goals, local emphasis and legislative focus are effective methods of attacking drug abuse.

Chapter 5

What the Three Pigs
Can Teach Us about Drug Abuse

Every day, it seems, brings reports of a new drug epidemic as well as reports of promising new research on drug abuse. If you're a parent, you can't escape. With all the new information out there—on television, in the newspapers, on the Internet—how do you know what to pay attention to and what to ignore? Will acupuncture cure addiction, as some researchers think? How about the New Age treatments of aromatherapy or crystals? As George Orwell might have said, some drug facts are more equal than others. Some are pure gold. Others are nonsense. This chapter will help you make sense out of the confusing world of drugs by providing a way to ferret out good information from the bad.

Knowledge about drugs and their effects is power. Drugs that can be grown in your backyard are more worrisome than one that must be imported. Knowing a little about a drug's chemistry can help you anticipate if an overdose is a minimal problem or a potential lethality. If you know what the effects of a drug are on your kid's body and mind, you'll be quicker to call a spade a spade and take timely steps to keep bad from going to worse. If you know a drug is habit forming, you'll have a set of responses which are different from those when the drug is not. This is medical knowledge, but don't leave it to your doctor to give you all the answers. Your doctor may be intelligent, well-trained and caring, but not necessarily an expert in all the things you need to know about drugs to keep your children safe.

In medicine some stuff is known much more solidly than other stuff. The best I call bricks and the least good, mud. To explain, let's take a look at the story of *The Three Little Pigs*. You know the headline version: Pig Defeats Wolf with Home Improvements. Now let's look at the story the way it really happened, from a medical point of view. We all know that each pig builds a house, one of straw, one of sticks and one of bricks. A wolf visits the first pig and with a massive, forced expiratory volume (you know, a big huff and puff), he destroys the straw house and eats the pig, overindulging himself in a meal of cholesterol and saturated triglycerides, contrary to the advice of his cardiologist.

He then visits the second pig, whose house is built of sticks and with another pneumonic blast blows the house down. This leads to a worsening of his serum cholesterol, fatty acid profile and a high degree of emotional overexcitement. His cardiologist orders a stress test, but the wolf is too busy to come in. Besides, he has one more visit to make to the third little pig.

When the wolf gets to the house of brick and tries the same high-pressured tactic with the third pig, he huffs and puffs until he collapses a lung. This leads to a drop in blood oxygen, a heart attack and the wolf's needless demise. The moral is that houses of brick are better than those made with lighter stuff.

Mud

For our purposes we can describe medical facts, like the building materials in the story, as falling into increasing levels of certainty: mud, straws, sticks and bricks. *Mud* is the stuff of clinical case reports. Now mud is cool, wet, good. It has many fine attributes. It holds together firmer stuff. In medicine, case reports turn our attention to promising new findings and encourage others to explore the findings with more definitive work. The vast majority of claims that marijuana has medicinal value fall into this category. Stephen Jay Gould, the eminent biologist, courageously reported on his beneficial use of marijuana during a period of cancer chemotherapy. Gould was one of the world's preeminent evolutionary biologists. He should know what he's talking about. Does this mean marijuana should be used to fight the nausea of chemotherapy? Perhaps, but more study is needed.

This is an endorsement, not a scientific fact. There are many limitations to endorsements and case reports. Science at its best is anti-authoritarian. Science turns on evidence. How good is the evidence of case reports? Not very, unfortunately. Media reports claimed that a compound from apricot pits, laetrile, could cure cancer. Untold numbers of desperate patients abandoned arduous conventional treatments and flocked to those who could provide this drug. Only after careful clinical studies was it shown that the claim was false. The drug had no anti-cancer effects in either animals or humans.

Similar case reports and unpublished medical claims are made every day. They number in the thousands. They are so numerous, in fact, that *refereed journals*, those in which articles are accepted for publication only after careful anonymous review by experts in their fields, have taken to discouraging case reports or limiting them to short letter formats. As untested claims, they form the bedrock of "alternative" medicine, now mushrooming into a popular and lucrative health care industry. Remember, though, that the bedrock is not rock at all, but mud. Such claims, whether they are treatments with magnets or Andean cacti, are alternatives to medicine and, until proven definitively, alternatives to reason.

Straw

This brings us to houses of straw, which are better than mud by far. In the world of human drug data, straw houses are analogous to *controlled comparison studies*. These are like horse races between two or more contestants. They answer the specific question, "Which horse is faster?" Such studies can be complicated and look at not only which horse is faster, but which diet (and dare I say drug?) correlates with faster horses. A typical drug study might be like one I conducted a number of years ago, in which a group of LSD users were compared to non-LSD using drug addicts to see if one group suffered more chronic visual hallucinations than the other. Indeed, as hypothesized, the LSD group more often described long-lasting visual hallucinations than the comparison group long after the LSD was discontinued. Data from this study were well received by psychiatrists. The findings became the clinical bedrock — that word again — for criteria for a new psychiatric disorder, Hallucinogen Persisting Perception Disorder (HPPD), enshrined in that Bible of psychiatric diagnoses, the Diagnostic and Statistical Manual of the American Psychiatric Association. Surely this is something that one can believe in, right? Well...perhaps.

Straw house studies like this one have limitations. Groups being compared may have true differences, but based not on the hypothesized variable, such as a drug being used, but on a variable not being studied at all. Many years ago, for example, a young researcher, who will remain unnamed, observed that patients developing psychosis after using hallucinogenic drugs tended to have blue eyes, compared to non-LSD using psychotic patients. This was very exciting and elaborate theories of brain chemistry were put together to explain this finding. But only after matching the two groups for age did he realize that the LSD group was considerably younger and more likely to be of Irish or English extraction, while the non-LSD group consisted of older, brown-eyed Italian-Americans. What was really discovered was that the LSD psychotic group was younger than other psychiatric patients (no big surprise) and of a different ethnicity than the non-LSD group.

Another mistake researchers can make is doing a study with too few people. In this case researchers often miss key differences between groups. Do certain drugs like Valium cause cleft palates in fetuses, for example? Since serious birth defects are rare, huge samples of cases need to be assembled to compare drug and non-drug groups in order to draw accurate conclusions. Huge samples are pricey. Pricey means hard to do. And hard to do often means we don't know. Even after studying thousands of babies, those exposed to Valium-type drugs *in utero* did not appear to be associated with birth defects any more than babies who weren't. These large, carefully done studies concluded that the drugs were safe for use in pregnancy. But were the samples large enough? Can we say Valium never causes cleft palates? A good clinician never says never.

Another problem is that comparison studies often look backward at what happened. This makes the acquired data hostage to the selective memory of the subject. In a study of the effects of marijuana taken in the past, for example, this raises problems. Did the study subject in question actually take marijuana? How do we know it wasn't angel dust or oregano? How do we categorize someone who used the drug "only once," but was not sure it was marijuana in the first place? Was the drug mixed with other drugs which could cause the hypothesized effect? Or was the subject in question too embarrassed or intimidated by the legal consequences of drug use to admit he used marijuana in the first place? These uncertainties introduce doubt that can weaken the conclusions of a straw house study.

Outcome variables of straw house studies may not always be reliable. Let's imagine that a researcher wants to know if marijuana is good for migraine headaches. Knowing that a testimonial from a single enthusiast is mud, she decides on a straw house strategy. She asks a hundred users of marijuana in a headache clinic a single question, "Does marijuana help your migraine?" Right away the study has a problem. To what is the researcher comparing the pot group? Suppose 50 percent of the sample reports the drug helps the headache. Does it help better than, e.g., aspirin? Is it safer than conventional treatments for migraine? Cheaper? The research doesn't tell us any of these things as the study is designed. The study has *no control subjects*.

There are further problems with straw house studies like our pot study for migraine. How do we treat answers other than yes and no? If a subject answers, "Awesome, dude!" you might conclude that pot helped. But what if the subject was being ironic? And how about ambiguous answers, like "Maybe," "I think so," and "Some of the time"? What if the researcher feels that marijuana should becomes listed as the Eighth Deadly Sin and is biased against a drug effect? Or what if the opposite is the case and the researcher sees marijuana as the key to peace on Earth? But in research, the Eighth Deadly Sin is not marijuana, it's bias. Bias shifts the interpretation of data one way or another. It requires constant vigilance to keep one's study free of bias. No study is perfect, but some are vastly better than others.

Finally, our headache study can run into other difficulties. The "pot" could have been another drug the user didn't know about. The "migraine" could have been another type of headache. Maybe the headache could have resolved without the use of pot and the report of "awesome" represented giving credit to marijuana for what Mother Nature did. Or the subject might have taken aspirin for the migraine an hour or two beforehand and not said so. The addition of a comparison group would help matters, but if the study did compare two groups, how could we be sure the groups were selected fairly? For example, it wouldn't be fair to compare a group of mild migraine patients who smoked pot with a group of severe sufferers who didn't, since the mild headache group would do better regardless of treatment type. You can begin to see how the casually designed study can give you, well, a headache.

The report of an "awesome" drug is good, no doubt about it. As a physician, I seldom challenge a patient's report that something which was safe also "worked." We have more ignorance about good treatments than knowledge. But good for what and for whom are harder questions to answer. There are many straw house studies in medicine. Some point the way to important advances in our knowledge. Others are waiting for their roofs to cave in.

Sticks

That brings us to houses of sticks, in general a great improvement over straw. Suppose you decide you're going to address the problem of bias by only recording unambiguous answers to standard questions, recorded by unbiased folks with no knowledge their data would some day be used in a scientific study. And suppose you create a control group to see if the study variable actually makes a difference in the first group's outcome. Alvin Feinstein at Yale University has called this kind of study a TROHOC study, "cohort" spelled backwards. That's because the TROHOC study takes a cohort of subjects and tries to find out what happened to them going back in time. These are not always easy studies to do. As a result, there are far fewer stick house studies than mud and straw studies.

One of my favorite stick house studies was done in 1979 by Thomas McLellan, George Woody and Charles O'Brien from the

University of Pennsylvania. They wanted to answer one of the more important questions in drug abuse. Namely, did specific forms of drug abuse lead to specific psychiatric illnesses? The team found a group of addicts who came to the same hospital each year to get the same standard psychiatric assessment. With a bit of scientific inspiration, they decided to arrange their cohort of drug addicts into three groups, depending on the patient's drug of choice. One group liked sedatives such as alcohol and tranquillizers. The second liked the stimulants amphetamines and LSD. And the third liked opiates like heroin.

What did they find? After six years of continued drug use, the group using downers had more depression, the group using amphetamines or LSD reported more psychosis and the opiate group remained unchanged. If these results were to be believed, the implications were that abuse of alcohol could lead to depression and the abuse of amphetamines or LSD could lead to madness — no small set of findings.

But thinking back on the limitations of straw studies, some of the same problems can be found in this remarkable contribution. We don't know for certain which drugs the subjects were taking or how open and honest they were in reporting drug use. Perhaps subjects who qualified in the alcohol group covertly used LSD a handful of times, became psychotic and actually weakened the study's conclusions. Or perhaps there were unnoticed differences in the lives of subjects over the six years that explained the results. For example, were the opiate addicts' lives stabilized with methadone maintenance, which then relieved depression they otherwise would have experienced? Was employment a factor or marriage? Or did some participants who had a genetic predisposition to psychosis prefer to use psychosis-making drugs in the first place? What can a parent conclude from even well-done studies? Answer: we don't know everything about anything, there is always room for error and always room for a better mousetrap.

Brick

Which brings us to houses made of brick: *prospective cohort studies.* These are solid scientific structures, hard to build, hard to take down and often becoming the foundation of fruitful work in parallel fields. Perhaps the most powerful and effective work of this type in the field of drug abuse was begun by Sir Richard Doll, Sir Austin Hill and others in the 1950s. These researchers asked a question the answer to which continues to be important a half century later: What if any harm is there to smoking cigarettes? Today the answers to this question—cancers and heart disease—are taken for granted by every American citizen except tobacco company executives. This wisdom did not come to us lightly, but as a result of a mountain of evidence brought to bear on the question.

Doll and Hill attacked the problem by collecting a cohort of doctors. The sample they studied started at 34,439 males in 1951, asking them periodically about their smoking habits and following them over time to see if smokers died sooner than non-smokers and from which diseases. Easy to say, hard to do. The main idea was, as the Brits would say, simply brill. Doctors were more likely to have stable addresses and families, more consistent health care, more careful diagnoses and more public recognition at death. (By comparison consider the problems of trying to study smoking in a cohort of homeless persons or migrant workers.) Another attribute these researchers had was patience. They followed the doctors for forty years.

The epidemiologists found that "about half of all regular smokers will eventually be killed by their habit." In the second half of the forty year span, the chance of dying for those doctors between forty-five and sixty-four years of age was increased three times for smokers and twice in the age span of sixty-five to eighty-four. Excess mortality was confirmed for cancers of the mouth, esophagus, pharynx, larynx, lung, pancreas and bladder; respiratory disease; vascular disease; peptic ulcer; cirrhosis; suicide; and poisoning. For this work Doll and Hill were honored with knighthood.

This classic study had lots going for it: large steady samples, high rates of responses to questionnaires and an epic span of time. Doctors, it appears, are particularly conscientious about returning health questionnaires. But not dead doctors. What if their final diagnoses were inaccurately entered into death certificates? How accurate were their families in describing what had happened? What if the families of doctors dying of smoke-related cancer were more committed to reporting their illness in the first place than healthy smokers who were indifferent to the effects of cigarettes? This could introduce a bias that inflated the number of tobacco-related deaths. (It should be noted that this study minimized this bias by relying on death certificates for the vast majority of its data, not family descriptions.)

However, bias is like flood water trying to seep into a house. There is one important remedy for this problem, which is the *placebo controlled, randomly assigned, double blind prospective study.* What this refinement provides for a brick house study threatened with high water bias seeping in is flood insurance.

Brick Houses with Insurance Policies

What insures against bias are: *controlled, randomly assigned and double* blind. Let's take them one at a time. *Controlled.* This means that you are trying to compare apples to apples and changing one condition to see if you get a different effect. When the effect of a drug is in question, a good control is to give one group the drug and a second group a placebo or inert compound and to then look for differences.

In an age when every drug is touted to be effective, only a few drugs do a small number of things very well. This attribute makes them possible candidates for medical use. Other drugs do lots of things. This is seldom good for people, since this is a good way to poison someone. Or a drug may do nothing at all, which is another problem. Comparing a drug effect to a placebo helps to answer the question of whether the drug (e.g. nicotine, marijuana, cocaine) results in a specific effect (e.g., cancer, pain relief, stroke). The downside of this strategy is that there are ethical limits to the use of test drugs and controls. The protection of human subjects must come before any scientific question.

So what are the concepts you should you look for when assessing any claim in the drug world?

Random assignment. Suppose we were to study the question of whether marijuana alleviates cancer pain, an important idea with humane consequences if true. And suppose by chance aspirin was the comparison drug and offered immediately after cancer surgery (ethically dubious, but arguable) in an ICU, while pot was offered to patients in a rehabilitation center overlooking a lake. Are the two settings comparable? No. Would they influence the outcome? More likely than not. You can see how unequal treatment of the two study groups could bias the outcome. How can this be remedied? One answer is to assign patients by chance to treatment in one group or the other randomly. This is a powerful way to take care of numerous sources of bias.

Double-blind is another way to insure a lack of bias. This means that in our theoretical marijuana study neither the research subject *nor the scientist who observes the outcome* knows which drug the subject received. This is another terrific insurance policy against bias.

Making sense out of medical data is tricky, but there is a scientist's *Guide de Michelin* for medical research, which will show you how to give a thumbs-up to valid scientific work.

TABLE 9: Comparative Strengths of Different Study Designs in Medical Research

Design	Strength = Number of Thumbs Up
Case reports	👍
Group comparisons	👍 👍
Group comparisons back in time	👍 👍 👍
Group comparisons forward in time	👍 👍 👍
Double blind, placebo controlled randomly assigned studies	👍 👍 👍 👍

There are many more subtle considerations in determining the value of a particular claim. But the table should help you get started in evaluating a study's value. In addition, useful signs of a serious medical research effort are:

- Large sample size
- Sensible idea, which relates well to previously demonstrated findings
- Lots of observations, reliably made
- Minimum of fuzzy math
- Effort by the researchers to understate the result

These ideals in medical research are difficult to achieve, as anyone who has tried can attest. They should be considered a hierarchy of progressive degrees of certainty about drug findings and, indeed, any other medical finding.

Take-Home Lesson #5

1) Not all drug facts are equal. Learn to evaluate the research.
2) Medical facts fall into increasing levels of certainty.
3) Random assignment and double blind studies remedy numerous sources of bias.
4) Despite advances in science, there is no magical formula to end or prevent drug abuse. It takes will, work and community.

Part II

Street Drugs:
Rap Sheets on the Suspects

Chapter 6

Tobacco: The Kids Are the Market

Tobacco is this country's number one lethal drug and the major gateway for kids moving on to other drugs. That is why a parent can make a big difference by turning the home into a smoke-free environment. This chapter tells you who and what you're up against, the rewards for winning the fight against tobacco and the costs of losing it.

Congress Invites the Tobacco Industry for a Sit-Down

Dr. John Slade, one of the pioneers who led the fight to get Americans to stop smoking, was trained in the study of epidemics. He was one of the first Americans to see tobacco advertisements as the key to the problem. "This is an infectious agent. This is the virus—these signs, this marketing." A 1962 internal memo retrieved from the files of Brown and Williamson, one of the world's largest tobacco producers, said as much: "We are in the business of selling nicotine, an addicting drug…" In the 1990s Congress began turning its attention to the practices of the tobacco industry.

Under the steady pressure of the medical profession, a series of anti-tobacco Surgeons General and a public which was progressively more educated about the dangers of tobacco, people began clamoring for more protection from the tobacco industry. In 1994 the country witnessed the spectacle of seven tobacco executives solemnly swearing under oath before Congress that nicotine was *not* addictive. In fact, smoking was no longer dangerous. When confronted about the links between smoking and cancer, Alexander Spears, Chairman of the Lorillard Tobacco Company, responded in 1997 that "nobody dies of cigarette smoking. You die of diseases." This was like a handgun enthusiast saying it's not the handgun that kills you, but the gunshot wound. The same year another Philip Morris executive told Congress that tobacco was no more addictive than the candy Gummi Bears, rivaling the whopper that Pinocchio told Gepetto. The comparison to Gummi Bears was apt, however. Gummi Bears are for kids and, it appears for Big Tobacco, so are cigarettes.

Kids Are the Market

Cigarette smoking increases the risk of subsequent use of marijuana and cocaine ten times. While the tobacco industry has denied the addictive potential of a clearly addictive substance, they have been expanding their markets and diversifying their holdings. In 1998 tobacco industry spent $6.7 billion to market cigarettes, the most heavily advertised consumer product in the nation. What is particularly distressing about their marketing strategy is how it blatantly targets the young.

A 1972 internal memo from RJ Reynolds reads, "The fourteen to eighteen year-old group is an increasing segment of the smoking population. RJR must soon establish a successful new brand in this market." RJR would later create the cartoon marketing character, Joe Camel. Besides the use of kid-specific branding, Congressional hearings uncovered that cigarette displays were placed near the doors of retailers. This enticed kids to steal them and then become dependent on them. Tobacco companies had learned what researchers had also concluded, which is that kids don't buy cigarettes half as much as they beg, borrow or steal them.

This disgraceful marketing tactic has been slow to come to the public's attention despite a series of wrongful death lawsuits leveled at big tobacco by states and health insurance companies in the last decade. Despite wide coverage and a number of settlements in the billions of dollars, one prominent 500-page textbook on adolescent drug abuse devotes a chapter to Satanism, but none to tobacco.

A Short History

Tobacco is one of the agricultural contributions that moved from the New World to the rest of the world. Native Americans used tobacco in every form, including that of rectal enemas, from Paraguay to Quebec. The sailor Juan Ponce de Leon brought the drug to Portugal. One of the Old World's first smokers, Rodrigo de Jerez, a member of Columbus' crew, was seen with smoke coming from his mouth in Europe. Fearing he was possessed by the devil, authorities jailed him for a year and a half. In 1565 Sir Walter Raleigh introduced smoking to England. From England, Spain and Portugal, traders carried the drug to Africa and Asia.

In the seventeenth century Turkey, Russia and China were sufficiently alarmed by the appearance of smoking in their countries that each imposed the death penalty for smokers. The Chinese decapitated tobacco dealers. The Romanov czars of Russia tortured and exiled smokers. Sultan Murad the Cruel, a man clearly indifferent to tobacco lobbyists of the time, executed many of his subjects for smoking (a punishment which, in light of modern medical research, appears unnecessary).

Governments since the seventeenth century have operated between the opposing forces of a desire to ban the addictive substance and a desire to reap the benefits of taxing it. In 1604 King James I published a "counterblaste to tobacco," but then set an import tax on it. In the 1980s the United States government was doing similar things, publishing Surgeons General's reports on smoking and collecting annual revenues of $5.5 billion in state and Federal taxes on tobacco sales. This apparent windfall for the government's coffers is offset by the estimated annual costs from smoking in the United States of $27 billion a year of medical care, absenteeism, decreased work productivity, accidents and the costs of other drug addictions promoted through tobacco use. It is not clear if this appeal to fiscal sense was at work, but a positive note in this otherwise sorry story is that the United States government, after opposing a World Health Organization treaty to control tobacco, changed its mind in 2003. In another bizarre twist to this story, as a result of liability litigation, cigarette companies currently distribute informative booklets on smoking prevention in kids. A glossy brochure from Philip Morris highlights a quote from the 2001 Columbia University Study, "Malignant Neglect," I could not agree with more: "Parents are the single most important influence on children's decision to smoke, drink or use drugs, yet many parents do not fully understand the extent of their influence." Yet one cannot escape the feeling that parents are being lectured on the Ten Commandments by the devil himself.

Tobacco Production

Washington Duke, a North Carolina farmer whose heirs later contributed to the building of Duke University, was the first to mass-produce cigarettes in 1884, "ushering in the era of cheap, abundant tobacco products for smoking and setting the stage for twentieth century epidemics of lung cancer, emphysema and coronary heart disease," as one expert succinctly put it. Duke's ability to mass-produce cigarettes resulted in a shift from cigars to cigarettes beginning in the last century. North Carolina and Kentucky continue to be the two largest tobacco producers in the United States. One fourth of the tobacco in a cigarette comes from tobacco scraps, that is, stems and previously discarded leaves, which are then ground up and mixed with many other ingredients.

Cigarette companies add nearly 600 different chemicals to their product, such as tobacco extracts, ammonia, corn silk and snakeroot oil, none of which is controlled by the FDA. Needless to say, tobacco remains big business. It's the sixth largest cash crop in the United States. Tobacco also means good business. The average pack of cigarettes costs about three cents to manufacture, giving a profit margin that rivals those of drug dealing and prostitution. Americans spend about $45 billion a year on cigarettes. What we have in the tobacco industry, in essence, is a legally sanctioned, socially destructive, highly profitable business that is politically connected and poorly regulated. Get the picture?

Who Smokes?

The good news is that fewer Americans smoke now than they did in the past, roughly a third of all adults. The bad news is that smoking is increasing in the rest of the world, especially in poor and emerging countries. And marketing to kids is working. Smokers are beginning earlier in adolescence both here and abroad. One study of the United States and Asian countries found that American kids start smoking sooner than kids elsewhere. On the other hand, good news from the Monitoring the Future Study is that there is a mildly favorable change in the long-term trend of kids willing to experiment with cigarettes. In the last twenty-five years those experimenters have dropped from 74 percent to 63 percent. In the last ten years the proportion of kids smoking at least half a pack per day stayed the same, 11 percent.

What's in a Cigarette: Cliffs Notes Version

First and foremost, cigarettes deliver tars and nicotine to the lungs. The average cigarette delivers about 1mg of nicotine and 12 mg of tar. Over 4,000 other substances have been identified in burning tobacco and paper, not many of which are likely to be good for you. Burning and inhaling tobacco creates an organic chemistry factory in a human being's lungs, producing, for example, tar, a sooty particulate, called the "complete carcinogen" in that it both causes and promotes cancers to grow. Nicotine and tar have received most of the bad press about the ingredients of cigarettes, but more evils from cigarettes are the radioactive isotopes of lead and polonium.

Polonium-210 has a half-life of 138 days, is a by-product of the extraction of radium from uranium minerals. Lead-210 has a half-life of twenty-two years. Each releases radioactive particles which can cause cancer. If a bit of lead-210 is absorbed into the lungs, the radioactivity will continue approximately 110 years, outlasting the average person's lifespan by several decades. As far as such radioactivity is concerned, you can run, but you can't hide.

Since 1950 the prevalence of lung cancer has been rising. Polonium is not an intentional additive of the cigarette industry. It is a by-product of atomic bomb blasts performed in the atmosphere since 1950 by American, Russian, British, French and Chinese nuclear weapons testing programs. It is not farfetched to think that this rare isotope found its way into tobacco from open air atomic bomb blasts. We know that smokers have more polonium in their blood than non-smokers. Hamsters, when given polonium, develop lung cancer at doses comparable to what smokers expose themselves to over a lifetime. The good news in this story is that quitting smoking is likely to let the lung significantly clear itself of polonium. The bad news is that filtered cigarettes do not adequately remove polonium and other substances from smoke and worse, being around someone who is smoking actually exposes you to *higher* levels of ammonia, nicotine and carbon monoxide than intentionally inhaled smoke.

What Cigarettes Do to You

Despite the fact that the amount of nicotine in cigarettes has lessened over the last forty years, cigarettes continue to be the biggest drug killer in America, ahead of alcohol, ahead of cocaine, ahead of heroin. They increase risk of premature death by 70 percent. Nicotine is an insecticide that acts with a speed comparable to that of cyanide. Were you to inject 60 mg of it — the weight of about 1/10th of a nickel — you would die in a rapid order of salivation, nausea, vomiting, diarrhea, weakness, confusion, coma and suffocation. There are 60 mg of nicotine in two cigarettes. So why, then, a wise kid may ask, don't you die if you smoke two cigarettes? Smart kid! But don't pass him a carton and a lighter just yet.

Why You Don't Die After Two Cigarettes

There are good reasons. First, people become habituated to the drug and are able to tolerate more of it over time. By contrast, no one starts a career as a smoker by smoking two packs of cigarettes the first day. On the other hand, someone new to tobacco can become ill with as little as 4 mg exposure to nicotine. Second, burning destroys much of the 20-30 mg of nicotine in a cigarette (while creating other chemicals that hurt the lungs). Third, if a little kid ate cigarettes (it's been known to happen, as any poison control center will tell you), he is protected from nicotine, because it's poorly absorbed in stomach acid. The drug slows its own absorption and causes vomiting, which gets rid of the poison before too much damage can occur. Good news for small children, but bad news if nicotine is used by other routes of administration, such as in rectal enemas for parasites, which has been fatal in the tropics. But, your kid may counter, she's not planning on eating cigarettes any time soon. So what's the problem?

Let's go back to our original idea that all drugs are poisons. Nicotine is an especially effective poison. When nicotine in inhaled in smoke it is taken into the brain within one to two minutes. Nicotine hits chemical receptors in the brain hard, increasing respiration, cardiac rate, blood pressure, oxygen consumption, blood vessel constriction and the release of fatty acids. Several ways smoking may contribute to heart disease are by straining the heart, narrowing arteries with plaque and reducing oxygen available to body tissues with carbon monoxide.

Getting hooked is the way in which a person lets cigarettes do their worst. One way nicotine addicts is that it releases dopamine in the brain's pleasure circuit involving the nucleus accumbens. This is a circuit also thought to be involved in the addictions to heroin, cocaine and alcohol. Heroin addicts who smoke (and most do), will tell you that quitting cigarettes is a lot tougher than kicking heroin. What makes kicking the habit so bad is the withdrawal syndrome of insomnia, irritability, anxiety, poor concentration, restlessness and generalized misery.

Long Term Medical Effects

Tobacco is the number one avoidable cause of death and disability in our society. It is the number one drug killer, ahead of alcohol. It's responsible for over 400,000 deaths a year and so gets top rating (Four Skulls) on our list of abusable poisons in chapter 1. To put 400,000 deaths a year in perspective, that number is six times the number of deaths at Hiroshima. Another way to look at it is that the tobacco industry drops the equivalent of six Hiroshima-sized atomic bombs on American citizens every year. The deaths come in many packages: heart disease, strokes, cancer, strangulating lung disease and stillborn infants of mothers who smoke. Fetuses that are born of smoking mothers are often underweight and at increased risk for peri-natal illness, learning defects and sudden infant death. Have I made my point yet?

As the facts of this bleak and distressing story have come together, the federal government under the leadership of a series of Surgeons General has attempted to regulate the tobacco industry. The 1964 landmark report of the Surgeon General concluded that "Cigarette smoking is causally related to lung cancer in men; the magnitude of the effects of cigarette smoking far outweighs all other factors." But the United States did not recognize tobacco use as an addiction until 1988. It took the government until the year 2000 to begin urging Americans to "reduce" tobacco use. Thus is the power of the tobacco lobby.

Addiction and Quitting

Perhaps the Surgeon General's idea of "reducing" tobacco use reflected a healthy respect for the addictive properties of tobacco. Its addictive potential is legendary. A nineteenth century wag once wrote that after reading of the effects of smoking, he was so horrified he gave up reading. Perhaps history's best known tobacco addict was Sigmund Freud, who smoked twenty cigars a day, could never quit and ultimately died of cancer of the throat. In the last one hundred years the data have mounted so that even entrenched addicts are try-ing to clean up. Some actually succeed. The relapse rates for smokers are roughly the same as those for alcohol and heroin addicts, roughly 80 percent within a year. Of those who can stick it out for a year, a third will pick up smoking at some point in the future. Tough odds for success, but not impossible.

One plus is that kids are more often than not on the toe of the curve of tobacco addiction, so that quitting is often easier and the outcome brighter. A large spectrum of behavioral and medical treatments is available. Tobacco avoidance behaviors, nicotine patches and gum all may help in quitting. In the case of multiple drug use or addiction, there is little merit in continuing to smoke cigarettes while cleaning up from other drugs.

The benefits of quitting are immediate and if relapse is avoided, long-lived. Carbon monoxide, a gaseous poison, is eliminated in twenty-four hours. In a few months, ex-smokers report less shortness of breath and cough. The senses of taste and smell return. Peripheral circulation improves. A dramatic example of benefit from quitting is that lungs, which had been gray or black from smoking, become a healthy pink again. The last great benefit to parents who make the fight over cigarettes is that they increase the chances of winning future fights over harder stuff, since for the kids who continue to smoke, other drugs lie in wait.

Take-Home Lesson #6

1) Cigarettes kill more people each year than any other drug, including alcohol.
2) Smoking is a major entrance point for kids moving to other drugs.
3) The tobacco industry must be stopped from marketing cigarettes to kids by print, television commercials and film.
4) Parents need to find ways to prevent their kids from starting to smoke cigarettes or work to get them to quit.
5) The benefits of quitting are immediate and long-lived.

Chapter 7

Marijuana: The Most Frequently Abused Illicit Drug in America

"Marijuana has never improved anyone's ability to do homework or hit a curve ball." Tom Hayden, Sixties Activist and California State Senator

Marijuana, Pot, Weed and Grass...

...are all the same substance. They are the leaves and flowers of the Indian hemp plant, Cannabis sativa, female gender. The gooey resin from the plant has at least 400 chemicals in it. It's the delta-9-THC (tetrahydrocannabinol) that has psychoactive properties, though there are probably others in the plant that do as well. The more THC there is in a given marijuana product, the greater the mental effects. Cultivated plants may comprise 1 percent THC. Oil derived from the resin (hash oil), may be as high as 60 percent. Bhang, another variety, found mostly in the United States, has 1-2 percent THC. ("THC" sometimes is used in reference to another smoked hallucinogen, phencyclidine, also called PCP. But marijuana is to PCP as a slingshot is to a sledgehammer.)

Ganja is another marijuana variant common in Jamaica, derived from flowers with high resin content. Hashish, a.k.a. hash, is derived mostly from resin and flowers. By now you are getting the point that marijuana goop and flowers are where the THC is found. Some varieties of pot, such as Sinsemilla, come from a potent Cannabis plant with THC as high as 10 percent. Given its worldwide usage, it is no surprise that the variations and potencies of the drug are great.

Worldwide Use throughout History

Ancient China first described the use of marijuana in a medical text. Medieval monasteries featured woodcuts of the plant, signaling its prominence in the lives of monks. Scholars speculate that the transcendent states of religious mystics may have been augmented by pot, which captured the imagination of nineteenth century European intellectuals, poets and physicians. At least one anthropological study has been done on Jamaican laborers who use the drug as a habitual part of their culture. Prior to World War II, marijuana use in the United States was found primarily among the wealthy, the underworld and entertainers. But in the 1960s marijuana involved all social classes and in particular became a countercultural symbol of rebellion against the Vietnam War.

Is Marijuana a Gateway Drug to Harder Stuff?

Yes, for some kids, but only a minority, marijuana use leads to the use of alcohol, LSD, cocaine and heroin. Studies show, however, that heavy pot use correlates with use of other harder stuff later on. For example, in one study kids who did not use pot had less than a 1 percent chance of heroin or cocaine later. However, kids who used pot more than 1000 times in their lives had a 33 percent chance of using heroin and a 73 percent chance of using coke. A second study found that kids who stayed off pot didn't use LSD later, but that 37 percent of the pot smokers ended up using acid.

It may also be that procuring pot connects kids to dealers who sell other drugs. Additionally, in certain kids one type of high creates an appetite for a greater high. Regardless of the sociology, the take home lesson is that if marijuana abuse or dependence is present, the chances of subsequent alcohol problems in a kid rise from 11 to 36 percent.

In the marijuana world of smoke and mirrors, scientific study of marijuana is overshadowed by the politics of marijuana. If the gateway theory is true, what does that say about legalizing the drug or using it for medical purposes? Nothing good. What it does say is that the generals and wardens conducting the war on drugs may have a point. And so a second look at the gateway theory may be in order.

This theory is not a popular item with the pro-drug crowd. Indeed, it's a favorite target. Despite good evidence by Golub and Johnson in 1994 showing that a majority of heroin and cocaine addicts used marijuana heavily before graduating to the harder stuff, Alison Mack and Janet Joy, researchers with the prestigious Institute of Medicine feel that such studies overinterpret the gateway theory. They argue that "Only a tiny fraction of the adult population — an estimated one to three per 1,000 people — uses crack or heroin [daily]. While most of the people interviewed for the [Golub and Johnson] study said they had used marijuana before moving on to harder drugs, that trend is not necessarily true among marijuana users in general." A point well taken. Crack and heroin have what epidemiologists call low attack rates and so, the argument goes, marijuana use is worth the risk.

Such reasoning prompts pro-drug activists to argue that for society as a whole the benefits of marijuana outweigh the risks. If a drug like penicillin can save many lives, but cause fatal allergic reactions in only a few, do we ban penicillin or take steps to use it more safely? Folks who argue for the medical use of marijuana are sympathetic to this line of thinking. However, the problem with this line of thinking is two-fold: 1) poor social controls are in place that increase the drug's safety; and 2) there are no firmly proven medical benefits of marijuana that are any better than drugs we already have on the market. Until these problems are solved, here are my Top Seven Kids Who Should Avoid Marijuana.

1) The kid at clear risk for use of harder drugs: This is the kid exposed to a range of genetic, family and personal risk factors than tip the scales in the wrong direction. Heavy pot use increases all the more the kid's risk of getting into harder drugs.

2) The kid with a history of run-ins with the law: The courts do not look kindly on repeat offenders, no matter what the offense. By far, legal entanglement is the greatest risk from marijuana for the majority of kids. Since 1965 there have been an estimated ten million arrests in the United States for marijuana-related offenses. Most marijuana laws are applied by the states. In my home state of Massachusetts, possession of any amount of pot is punishable by six months' jail time and a $500 fine. First offenders who are minors may escape jail and be placed on probation. But the risk of fines, legal fees, property loss, prison and a criminal record is not negligible.

3) The kid who has developed psychological dependence on marijuana: This kid smokes every day or so whether or not he needs it. As I discuss in the section "Is Pot Addicting?" the short answer is that it's not. But the kid who is smoking every day is doing so for a reason and seldom is the reason a good one. Better to find out the reason and address it than look the other way.

4) The kid who self-medicates with pot for an undiagnosed psychiatric disorder: This kid knows something is wrong with himself, but doesn't have the insight to identify the early signs of depression, anxiety or psychosis. Smoking dope in this instance may be a way to make painful emotions and thoughts go away for awhile.

5) The kid with visual problems after using LSD: There is a chance this kid is developing HPPD, hallucinogen persisting perception disorder (see chapter 9, "Acid: The Good, the Bad and the Permanent"). Anyone developing these persistent visual disturbances is likely to see them intensify by using marijuana. Such worsening can be long-lived or permanent. My advice to the kid with this problem who is around pot? Run!

6) The kid with a pre-existing psychosis: In this situation, a kid has suffered a psychotic illness, such as schizophrenia or manic-depressive illness, is helped with psychiatric treatment and then goes to a party and returns home with a psychotic relapse. Drugs that appear to do this are stimulants like cocaine and amphetamines, the hallucinogen LSD and marijuana.

7) The kid addicted to other drugs: This is the kid who battles to stay clean every day. What marijuana does here is to dissolve the kid's vigilance and set the stage for relapse. I can't count the number of addicts who told me their relapse began with a single joint (or drink).

In the meantime, the gateway theory clearly is not the whole explanation for the complexities of drug addiction. The data, though, speak for themselves. Kids who use pot heavily are at greater risk for later use of heavy drugs. Period. On the other side of the coin, some kids can skip over the step of pot abuse and graduate to careers in heroin or cocaine. Heavy pot use is not required for subsequent addictions to take hold, it just increases the odds.

Who Smokes?

The short answer is that kids in both junior high and high school smoke. Among eighth graders, use rose from 10 percent in 1991 to 20 percent in 2001. That was quite a jump. In 1991 23 percent of all tenth graders experimented with marijuana. Ten years later that number was 40 percent. The long-term trends among twelfth graders show a stable pattern of lifetime use of marijuana from 41 percent in 1990 to 49 percent in 2001. Daily pot use within the last thirty days among twelfth graders, the most worrisome pattern of use, like that in eighth graders, tripled from 1991 to 2001.

Why is this happening? Here are a few possibilities: First, a certain degree of "generational forgetting" may be going on, in which the current group of kids fails to learn from the mistakes of the preceding generation of kids who used pot. Second, despite programs like D.A.R.E., there is a decline, or disbelief, in drug education. How accurate and well-presented are the drug use lessons in classrooms, when they are present at all? Therein lays the tale of a societal failure.

Simple queries of drug education programs in your community may provide answers to some important questions: 1) Does drug education go on in the first place? 2) What are the qualifications of the teacher? 3) Where does the information in the course come from? 4) Do the kids believe it? And 5) Do the kids believe they are learning something? Call your local school, talk to teachers, administrators and counselors and talk with your child. Two other factors which may explain the increase in pot use among the young are a gradual sanctioning of pot for medicinal use and an upward trend in cigarette smoking among the young in the last decade.

It's the pattern of pot use to which a parent should be alerted. Many kids will try marijuana. Daily use is the doorstep to a wasted life. It's good to know the difference. While pot is the first illicit drug chosen in the life cycle, its use can facilitate the path to the next illicit drug. However, ritualistic use of pot in groups of occasional users is seldom a red flag. Dope becomes worrisome when a kid begins to turn to it on a daily basis to relax, get through the day, beat back depression or use it to establish an identity. An even worse case scenario is when a kid begins to use pot to modify effects of other drugs such as cocaine or alcohol.

Is Pot Addicting?

For those who want a quick answer, the answer is no. For those who want the whole truth, the answer is yes. (It pays to read the complete story.) Let me explain with a few definitions.

Drug Abuse: A pattern of troubling drug use occurring within the same twelve-month period but less encompassing than drug dependence, characterized by less than three of the following: interference with major life roles, use in hazardous circumstances, recurrent legal problems and continued use despite the above. The kid who gets cited for driving under the influence qualifies for this diagnosis or who uses dope daily and drops out of high school.

Physical Dependence: A drug-related set of symptoms occurring in a matter of hours to days following the cessation of a drug. Not all drugs cause this to happen. Classically addictive drugs are the usual suspects: nicotine, alcohol, heroin, cocaine. This also can happen to anyone who develops tolerance to medically prescribed pain medications and then stops taking them after a week or two. It also can happen if a drinker suddenly stops binging on alcohol.

Drug Dependence (also called Behavioral Dependence: A pattern of dysfunctional use of a particular drug over a twelve-month period, which includes at least three of the following:

- drug tolerance (taking more to get the same effect)
- withdrawal (getting sick on stopping the drug)
- increasing drug consumption
- persistent desire or repeated failures to cut down or stop
- lots of time spent getting the drug
- giving up important school or social activities to use the drug
- drug use despite knowledge it is causing a problem

Clearly the drug dependent kid is a kid in trouble. This is addiction, but not as bad as it sounds, to my way of thinking, since addicted kids have a fighting chance to kick the habit as well and in some ways, better than their adult counterparts.

Now let's put marijuana in perspective with other abusable drugs. Using the list of drugs from our Clinical Worry Index in Table 2, let's compare them in terms of their ability to result in the above conditions of Abuse, Physical Dependence and Behavioral Dependence. Table 10 summarizes this discussion. Black Clouds note which drugs cause which conditions. Little Clouds denote smaller, but not negligible, effects in that column.

TABLE 10: Black Clouds Of Drug Dependence

	Abuse	Physical Dependence	Behavioral Dependence
Tobacco	■	■	■
Alcohol	■	■	■
Heroin	■	■	■
Amphetamines	■	■	■
Cocaine	■	■	■

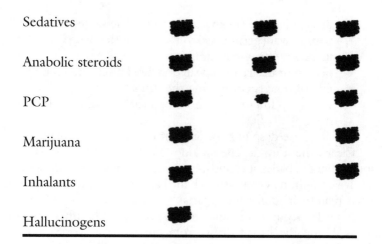

Sedatives

Anabolic steroids

PCP

Marijuana

Inhalants

Hallucinogens

Note that marijuana is *not* associated with physical dependence. True enough, but pot can still get kids into trouble. It's just that the trouble is not likely to be in the same league as that of kids using tobacco, alcohol or crack. Kids seldom experience tolerance and withdrawal when using marijuana. Kids rarely devote their lives to smoking weed, at least while living with their parents. That is not to say that there is no possibility of craving marijuana once use is ended. In fact, pot raises the interesting wrinkle that even as it does not cause withdrawal, it can nevertheless lead to behavioral dependence. Dependence on marijuana can occur with use over a matter of days. The lifetime risk for dependence is estimated at 10 percent, compared to alcohol (15 percent), opioids (23 percent) and tobacco (32 percent).

Clinical signs of kids' dependence on marijuana include: spending time trying to score pot, spending increasing amounts of money to pay for it and dropping out of the usual activities of kids, like sports, socializing, musical studies, school — anything that takes a certain amount of mental focus. I don't encourage a parent to wait for these worrisome signs to appear, nor depend on them before intervening. They are late stage warnings in the natural history of marijuana abuse and dependence. Intervening in the earlier stages of experimentation has higher success rates. So what is most helpful? Let's imagine that your kid, yes, *your* kid, is going to a party with friends where drugs are likely to precede, if not replace, the Doritos.

These are a few basics for Heads-up Parenting. Think of them as four phases, with each phase needing a different approach. Let's call Phase 1 Before the Party.

Before the Party

This is the most obvious and yet in many ways the most difficult thing for a parent to do: know your child. It's difficult because teens are moving targets, physically, intellectually, behaviorally and psychologically. Each passing moment in time means that you are losing control over what they do, where they go and who they hang with. It's a healthy thing, but not without its dangers. It's also not such a healthy thing, when parents work long hours to make ends meet and kids are left to fend for themselves. But knowing your kid is the heart of Heads-up Parenting.

So before the party, think in terms of a kid's baseline. How alert is he? What is her baseline mood like? How responsive is she to ordinary conversation? How able is he to think on his feet, use common sense and solve problems? These are tall orders in the best of circumstances, since the spirits of kids rise and fall in a pattern that could add a new chapter to chaos theory. Remember, trying to know your child's moods and mentality is better than not trying. So off she goes to the party, as you quietly say a prayer in the religion of your choice. This brings us to Phase 2.

Listening to Stoned

Chances are you will not be invited to this party. But you can imagine it. You may already have been there: the laughter, the music, the smell of dope in the air, turning the living room or game room or whatever into a dimly lit den of teenage hormones and the distinct smell which is one part acrid, two parts sweet and one part barn. Now let's don our Invisible Parent Outfit and drop in unexpectedly and unseen.

At this party, in the kids' heads there will be the experience of time drifting by. There will not be much dancing going on. The kids will be passive. And if you track conversation, you may notice repetitions in speech, evidence of failing short-term memory. Conversations like "Gimme the Twinkies, Dude." "You just ate the Twinkies." "No I didn't." "Yes, you did," followed by laughter.

Conversations themselves will be disjointed and often aimless. The order of the evening is to be happy while being given permission to be stupid, the central appeal of dope. And so the mood in the room will be elevated, dreamy and mirthful. Ideas may become playful and language will be marked with an increase in paradox and puns. This brings us to Phase 3.

Right after the Party

Back home, you will not have all this insider information. And so how can you tell if your kid has been smoking pot? The best way to find out if your kid has been using is simply to ask. On some level most kids want you to ask. It means you care. Hug him. Smell him. Let him know what you're doing. Of course, you may not have this opportunity. He may still be at the party. He may call home stoned. Number one on my Top Ten Things to Say When Your Kid Calls Home Stoned list is "I'll come and get you and your friends, too, if they need a ride."

The biggest danger statistically in being stoned, besides the predations of the legal system, is poor judgment and reduced skills in driving. Worse, of course, is that often a kid will mix pot and alcohol which markedly increases the chance of a fatal outcome. It will not do any good for a parent to play Grand Inquisitor at this point. Remember, dope reduces short-term memory and reading the riot act to a kid who is under the influence of a drug is like kicking him when he's anesthetized. It's unfair and unproductive. But having a policy of picking your kid up anywhere, anytime, with no questions asked, is Heads-up Parenting.

Picking her up from the party is also a golden opportunity to meet your child's friends and hopefully, other parents. Undue mirth at parting is a flag, but after all, she's coming from a party. However, barny smell, red eyes and a giddy, illogical brain may tip you off. Signs of unexpected panic or paranoia will also be clues. (A urine screen for drugs at the pediatrician can be positive for THC a month after last use.) This brings us to Phase 4, The Day After.

The Day After

This is the time for a Sit Down. True hysteria is seldom useful. Setting limits is better. One parent's limit setting may not be another's and being true to your own parenting style is likely to be best. One of my favorite anti-smoking speeches that a parent used began, "You will never be permitted to smoke in this house. If you try to smoke outside of the house, I will smell your clothes whenever you come home. I will search your room for lighters and tobacco. If I find evidence of smoking tobacco or dope or smoking paraphernalia, I will destroy the dope and the paraphernalia and ground you. If you try to smoke after school, I will drive around town looking for you and if I find you smoking you will be grounded twice as long. You will not get away with it!"

This kind of speech really impresses teenagers that you are serious, assuming you don't talk this way as a rule. The downside is that any healthy, self-respecting kid will be tempted after hearing it to test that limit and see if he *can* get away with it. You can try a similar speech, but it has to be convincing. In general I don't recommend this type of speech. I suggest rational concern backed up by information. Share the data — the good stuff — on tobacco, lung disease and pot as a gateway to harder stuff. "Not everything you hear about drugs is true, but this is the best information I can give you right now..." And here it is.

Adverse Effects of Marijuana:
When You're Stoned and When You're Straight

Kids focus on the fun side of being stoned. On the downside are 1) panic attacks, 2) paranoia and 3) impaired driving skills. The first makes you think that you are dying when you're not. The second makes you think you're at risk of being killed. The third actually can kill you. Not every panic attack makes you feel you're going to die. Some just make you feel you're losing your mind. These don't happen to everybody, but they can happen to anybody and that's the risk. Who needs it?

One important long-term effect of marijuana is that it clearly increases the chances of future use of more dangerous drugs such as alcohol, cocaine and heroin. It's important also to recognize that this is more likely to occur in heavy users of pot, not casual ones. However, good research has nailed down this gateway effect. People who argue against this effect are largely folks who want the drug legalized and probably those who want to sell it like tobacco.

Heavy users sometimes report the loss of the quality high, so that over time peacefulness, relaxation and the subjective impressions of increased mental powers are replaced with paranoia, anxiety and discomfort leading to less drug use. Many say they still like marijuana and would use it more often, but they can't tolerate the drug's psychological effects. Among them are subtle impairments in memory, attention and organization of complex information.

How can some kids skip school after earlier perfect attendance? Answer: they now smoke dope heavily. That's because pot reduces mental function. The more you smoke, the worse it gets. At a certain point, a kid who is a heavy smoker will be in school in body only. Of especial vulnerability is the ability to remember words. Since learning involves language much of the time, the marijuana user in school is taking on the job with a self-imposed mental handicap. If he smokes on Sunday, Tuesday and Thursday, chances are his mental abilities will be affected on Monday, Wednesday and Friday, as well as the rest of the week. In other words, the impaired cognitive effects of marijuana last longer than the time of the high. Some studies report that in heavy smokers who stop, mental abilities are reduced for as long as a week after stopping.

The good news is that as the THC in the body begins to clear, so does the brain. But what happens to the kid who smokes regularly while in school? He misses school while sitting in the classroom. And missing school is a gate to harder drug use, poorer jobs and ultimately economic disenfranchisement. This is what used to be called the "amotivational syndrome" of marijuana. It occurs with heavy use, but is reversible with sobriety. One big question among academicians has been, "Do slacker boys gravitate to dope or does dope make for slacker boys?" The answer for the Heads-up Parent is: Who cares? It's a two-way street that you don't want your kid on, no matter in which direction he's moving.

Other long-term effects of smoking dope include chronic bronchitis and cell changes in the lung indicating a pre-cancerous condition. Certain cancers which are exceedingly rare in younger people, e.g. cancer of the tongue, seem to be found more in pot smokers. It's also clear that kids suffering from schizophrenia become worse after using pot.

Much less certain are whether using marijuana lowers testosterone, reduces sperm counts or lowers the birth weights of babies. Similarly, it's not proven that pot use by parents retards the neuropsychological development of babies or increases their risk of cancers. And finally, there is no association with gross structural brain damage or violent or accidental deaths, despite a proven effect on driving. This last paradox may be explained by the disproportionate number of alcohol related accidents and acts of mayhem, which overshadow accidents related to dope. Finally, there is no longer the threat of paraquat poisoning from contaminated dope, since the federal government ended this disreputable practice of spraying marijuana crops with the herbicide following a public outcry over 9,000 paraquat related illnesses. Crops are now sprayed with another weed killer.

Throughout any battle a parent has with a kid over marijuana, it's important to take it seriously and treat the problem with passion, but take comfort in the fact that most kids do not destroy their lives with marijuana. Anne Roiphe, the novelist and mother, observed, "The difference between moderate experimentation and catastrophic drug taking is vast." And Richard Evans, a pro-marijuana activist, gave this advice to his young son: "You will one day be invited to smoke marijuana. I want you to decline. However, if you try it, I want you to remember that the harm of any drug is only partly due to the drug itself. More important are the physical, social and psychological circumstances…in the case of marijuana the greatest harm comes from being arrested." Of equal concerns for parents is the increased long-term risks of addiction tobacco and hard drugs, lung disease, the degradation of a kid's education and the worsening of schizophrenia and other mental illnesses.

The Marijuana Lobby

In 1999, the prestigious Institute of Medicine issued a report prompted by political pressure to legalize marijuana for a variety of medical conditions. In addition to a careful review of the scientific literature — the usual way such work is done — the authors also conducted public workshops, invited patient presentations, visited cannabis buyers' clubs and consulted with scientists and 130 organizations. They also took the creative, if scientifically meaningless, step of inviting comments on the topic using a public website. I feel this is a good example of what Dr. Virchow meant when he said that social science, when written large, is politics, since whatever the Institute came up with would affect the politics of marijuana. Here is a summary of the study's conclusions:

Marijuana possibly has uses in fighting nausea, for example, from cancer chemotherapy. It may stimulate appetite in AIDS patients. It may also be helpful in chronic pain in cancer, migraine, cord injury, stroke and nerve injury. Although experimental pain did not show a good pot effect, cancer patients getting the higher doses of THC had less pain than those getting low or no THC. Unfortunately, there was only weak evidence that THC could help multiple sclerosis or cord injury. There was the least benefit for glaucoma, seizures and anxiety.

One of the main problems with the medical use of marijuana is that you have to smoke it. Another is that in order to get the medical benefits, consciousness is altered. This may not be too different from prescribing a narcotic to treat pain, but the main goal of the treatment is not to create euphoria, but to relieve suffering. Put another way, a doctor should not be a bartender. These sentiments were not lost in the final report. These issues could be addressed by scientists developing smokeless delivery systems and sculpting from the compounds of the marijuana plant molecules that, for example, relieved pain without clouding consciousness. The Report concluded, "Whole marijuana is not a modern medicine."

On the Social Control of Marijuana

For any policy choice, no matter what type, it's useful to remember that some will benefit and some will pay. Keep that in mind and everything gets easier when we consider the social control of pot. Three options to consider: the first is criminalization of marijuana use. This is what we do now. It's been a good deal for smugglers, growers, dealers and the "corrections" industry, since the game of cops-and-dealers drives the price of pot up and fattens the budgets for law enforcement. It is not a good deal for "criminals," many of whom are imprisoned with long sentences for nonviolent crimes. It's also not a good deal for taxpayers, who pay for the expansion of America's number one growth industry of the last decade, the prison system. Criminalization reduces drug use somewhat, but with long, porous borders both north and south in the United States, it's no surprise that marijuana is still likely to be found in every school lunchroom in America.

The second option is legalization. Although the medical benefits from marijuana would likely be negligible, pot users would be happier and more numerous. Fewer, if any, would go to jail needlessly. Medical research into possible benefits of cannabinoids could be conducted. The greatest social costs from this option would be from increased drug use: both acute and long-term, as well as the collateral damage of other drug abuse.

The numbers of users would be large, as would the numbers of those with drug complications. In California, for example, legalizing the medical use of the pot attracted 12,000 members in one San Francisco club alone. It is likely this scenario would be played out nationally. It is possible there is an as yet unproven medical benefit for marijuana in patients suffering from AIDS, cancer or chronic pain. But there would most certainly be a push for the recreational status of pot and the commandeering of the market by the tobacco industry. We would, however, reduce the currently obscene costs of the criminal justice system, which drain revenues away from badly needed non-military budget items. We would also benefit from a reduction of the drug-driven police state.

The last option is the one that I favor, namely, the decriminalization of marijuana use. While it appears that in states where this has already occurred, marijuana use may have increased, while use of harder drugs has *decreased*. As Karyn Model, a RAND researcher tentatively concluded from her 1993 national study of drug related ER visits, "results suggest that some substitution occurs towards less severely penalized drugs when punishments are differentiated." Translated for the rest of us, what the RAND researcher found was that people will shift to use more marijuana *and less hard stuff* if the marijuana penalties are reduced. This is the model of reducing drug abuse through substitute dependence.

Thus, there is the risk of a social cost of increased pot use with this option, but social gains in reduced law enforcement and prison expenses. This policy has already been put to the test in the Netherlands, which decriminalized pot use in 1976. In a multi-year study of the effects of this policy, researchers found little support for the idea that pot use increased, *until* sale of the drug became commercialized in Dutch coffee houses! If true, the safest thing to do if pot is decriminalized, it would appear, is to keep it out of the hands of the cigarette companies.

Removing the penalties from pot use is likely to increase the realization that drug abuse is a medical disorder, not a crime. As Jocelyn Elders, former United States Surgeon General, said, "If drug use were to be viewed primarily as the medical problem it is, we would have more resources for preventing and treating drug addiction instead of spending most of our money criminalizing use, which has had virtually no effect at all."

Moving pot out of the courts and into the clinics is likely to stimulate medical research into possible benefits of the molecules of marijuana. At the present time, however, I believe there is nothing medical that marijuana can do that can't be done better by drugs already on the market.

Take-Home Lesson #7

1) Heavy pot users are at greater risk for poor school performance and the use of harder drugs than other kids.
2) Top Seven Kids who should avoid pot: those who have psychological dependence on pot, those who are at clear risk for use of harder drugs, those who have had run-ins with the law, those who self medicate, those who have visual problems after LSD and those who have pre-existing psychosis or are addicted to other drugs.
3) A serious danger from marijuana for the majority of kids is getting arrested.
4) Marijuana as medication does not work as effectively as legal medications already on the market.
5) Drug use should be decriminalized and treated as a medical disorder.

Chapter 8

Alcohol: The Rite of Passage

Hazing at Chuck's fraternity, Klan Alpine, was a time-honored tradition, a ritual as old as trial by fire and the maturation rites of primitive tribes. And so Chuck allowed himself along with two other pledges the night of their initiation to be locked into the trunk of a car. Beforehand, the three boys were allegedly given a pint of liquor, a six-pack of beer and a quart of wine and ordered to drink it all in the trunk by the time the car had ended its drive. Afterwards, the pledges were required to drink more alcohol back at the fraternity house. When Chuck passed out, he was carried upstairs and left on a mattress where, according to the coroner's report, he stopped breathing a short while later. The coroner diagnosed the cause of his death as alcohol poisoning.

As this painful story illustrates, alcohol can kill your kid in hours. Any family member of an alcoholic can tell you it can also kill him over a much longer span of time. So the kid who starts drinking risks both the quick consequences of abuse as well as the long-term slide into alcohol addiction. Because alcohol is available, advertised and symbolized as a mark of sophistication, alcohol is one of the first drugs to be tried on the teenage hit parade. One eighth grader in five has tried alcohol in the last thirty days. This is about twice the prevalence of an eighth grader's use of tobacco and vastly higher than the use of any other drug in that age group. In other words, tobacco and alcohol are the first addictive substances a thirteen-year-old is going to run into in the no good world of drug abuse. Of the two, alcohol is going to be used more often.

That's because, as I noted earlier, most kids who have drug careers begin with drugs that are legal and available. Alcohol serves multiple roles for a teenager: social lubricant, dissolver of angst, milestone of maturity. Remember though, kids do not consume alcohol the way adults do. Kids tend to drink to get drunk. However, being drunk on multiple occasions is a slippery slope. Unlike marijuana, the addictive properties of alcohol are universally recognized and the consequences of the addiction are devastating not only to the drinkers, but to anyone who loves, hires, teaches or sits beside them in a car. From a medical point of view, alcohol mis-use continues to be one of our more devastating social diseases.

Healthy kids are experience seekers. Alcohol fills that need. Being drunk is an experience, one that kids are told is grand, exhil-arating and important by poets and the liquor industry alike. Being drunk together fosters rapid if short-lived bonds between kids by dissolving the faculties by which we make discriminating judgments about ourselves and others. The most dangerous use of alcohol among the young occurs in colleges, when kids are free of parental constraints and counselors, professors and administrators are look-ing the other way. The use of alcohol among the young is particu-larly pernicious when one considers how they are targeted by the liquor industry. Craig Garfield, Paul Chung and Paul Rathouz at the Northwestern University published a study in 2003 analyzing the alcohol ads of thirty-five major magazines in the United States. Striking was that with each increase in the number of adolescent readers, there was an increase in the number of ads for beer and liquor (though not for wine). Obviously the ads do what the com-panies intend. Consider the findings of Susan Foster and colleagues from Columbia University, who calculated in a 2003 report that in the U.S. in 1999 $116 billion were spent on alcohol — $22.5 bil-lion of which was by kids between the ages of twelve and twenty.

Booze on Campus

Although drinking is illegal for most college students, a study of 14,000 college kids in 2000 by Henry Wechsler and Meichun Kuo at the Harvard School of Public Health found that 35 percent of all students engaged in binge drinking. These are big numbers and big time risks for your college-aged kids.

The National Institute on Alcohol Abuse and Alcoholism provides a punch list of the consequences of the drinking on campuses.

- **Death:** 1,400 college students between the ages of eighteen and twenty-four die each year from alcohol-related unintentional injuries.
- **Injury:** 500,000 students are unintentionally injured under the influence of alcohol.
- **Assault:** More than 600,000 are assaulted by other students who have been drinking.
- **Sexual Abuse:** More than 70,000 students are victims of alcohol-related sexual assault (making alcohol, the number one date-rape drug).
- **Unsafe Sex:** 400,000 students had unprotected sex and more than 100,000 students report having been too intoxicated to know if they consented to having sex.
- **Academic Problems:** About 25 percent of college students report academic consequences from their drinking.
- **Health Problems/Suicide Attempts:** More than 150,000 students develop alcohol-related health problems, including suicide attempts.
- **Drunk Driving:** 2.1 million students drove under the influence of alcohol.
- **Property Damage:** More than 25 percent of administrators from schools with low drinking levels and over 50 percent from schools with high drinking levels say their campuses have "moderate" or "major" problems with alcohol-related property damage.
- **Alcohol Abuse and Dependence:** 31 percent of college students met criteria for the diagnosis of alcohol abuse and 6 percent for alcohol dependence in the prior twelve months.

Thankfully, some school officials are waking up. Called the nation's "Number One Party School" by the Princeton Review in 1994, the University of Rhode Island has made a serious effort to educate kids going to its school. The number of college administrators willing to take strong stands against illegal alcohol use on campus is small but growing. Edward A. Malloy, president of the University of Notre Dame, noted recently that 95 percent of disciplinary action has been related to alcohol and its abuse and breeds what he calls "a culture of irresponsibility."

Ironically some college presidents have limited ability or courage, to control alcohol on their campuses. I asked one college president if he had considered making his school a dry campus:

"We could never do that," he said. "It would cut into our applications."

Under the leadership of the National Alcohol Institute, NIAAA, fifty-four colleges now publish their alcohol and drug policies on a government sponsored website, *http://www.collegedrinkingprevention.gov/policies/*. This permits Heads-up parents to find and discuss with their kids if the colleges to which he or she is applying 1) has a policy on drugs and alcohol; and 2) whether the policy is any good. A terribly important question for parents with college bound kids: Is this a safe place to send my child for the next four years?

Kids Who Booze

As I said previously, the kid heading into trouble with drugs and alcohol starts, more often than not, heading that way before college is in the picture and often in place of college. The majority of all kids, by the time they reach their senior year in high school have tried alcohol. But the most worrisome are the kids who drink in binges. Twenty-five percent of all twelfth graders report binge drinking as recently as the last two weeks. This is not a good number. The same is true for 15 percent of eighth graders.

Needless to say, booze is everywhere. Nearly 100 percent of twelfth graders report that alcohol is "easy" to get. The same is true for what 70 percent of eighth graders say. Half of all high school seniors report using alcohol in the last thirty days, with a third of all seniors reporting being drunk in that time. And what is the result of this casual acceptance of alcohol as a part of teenage life? A setting of the stage for the commonest causes of death of males between twenty and forty: accidents, homicide, suicide and cirrhosis. Thus, the news stories of parents who came to grief by letting their daughter and friends have a party with "controlled drinking" in their family room—only to have it end in a fatality when one of the kids tried to drive home himself—is frequent.

There are economic costs as well, estimated at eighty-five billion dollars a year. People who most benefit from alcohol are the liquor and entertainment industries and politicians who receive campaign contributions from the liquor lobby. People who pay are the rest of us. There are twenty-five million alcoholics in the United States, forty million relatives and other innocent victims of alcoholics and a straining health care system that pays for the management of diverse alcohol related diseases of the throat, stomach, liver, pancreas, brain and nerves.

Insurance companies end up paying, too, because of alcohol-related accidents and injuries and then pass the costs on to us, the consumers. Finally, bringing this full circle, the kids who booze become employees whose employers pay because of decreased productivity in the workplace. They deal with this by firing these young alcoholics and sending them on their way down the economic spiral.

Alcohol and Your Kid's Brain

Let's take a closer look at fifteen-year-old Mickey, as he and his friends imbibe a case of beer, purchased for them legally by a disheveled man near the liquor store in return for money the boys give him for a six pack of his own. For this thought experiment we will use an imaginary camera that lets us follow a molecule of alcohol through the fifteen year old's body.

Mickey's mom and dad are out to dinner with friends. The kids have been left to their own devices. Our stat alcohol molecule, or as he would be called on *The Simpsons,* "Mr. Al Cohol Molecule," is in for a big night: where will he end up? Stomach? Liver? Brain? Puke? It's all pretty exciting for a little guy who's just spent eight weeks in the can.

Mickey's getting a little woozy, since food slows the absorption of our molecule in the GI tract and he hasn't eaten dinner yet. Most of the alcohol is broken down in his liver, but because Mickey's a kid, those liver enzymes are immature, so more is getting to the brain than would in an adult. Our little Mr. Molecule finds his way to Mickey's brain within minutes.

Once there it blocks the NMDA brain receptors that help you stay alert and responsive, which means that your kid is becoming dull and dopey. Mr. Molecule then slams into a second brain receptor, GABA. This receptor makes him feel calm, brave and indifferent to danger, such as the sound of his Dad's car pulling into the driveway. This effect of Mr. Molecule is like the effects of a tranquilizer plus. It's the reason the folks in AA say that taking those drugs is "eating your booze." It's the reason that drunken fish in a lab tank fight more than sober ones. It's also the reason that when a person soaks his brain in alcohol for five or more days and then stops drinking, these two receptors are thrown into a chaotic pattern of over- and under-activity, resulting in memory problems, seizures and brain damage (thankfully rare in fifteen year olds).

What is not unlikely, though, is that Mr. Molecule is also traveling to a part of the brain that serves as a reward center. Mickey is learning, courtesy of the little molecule, that alcohol is fun, a *reward* in its own right. But the brain is also learning to tolerate the little molecule and to seek ever-larger numbers of our little molecule's friends to get the same effect. This is tolerance, never a good sign. Can fifteen-year-olds develop tolerance? Yes. Ultimately, a tolerant addict will use the drug of choice, such as alcohol, not to feel pleasure, but to feel *normal.* But that's for the future. Right now the car door slams and as Mickey's parents enter the house you hear the clatter of kids and cans in the basement and the classic, overly cheerful greeting, "Hi, Mom! Hi, Dad! What are *you* doing home?"

Bad Medical Stuff from Alcohol

How can so simple a molecule as alcohol (it has only two carbon atoms!) have such widespread effects in the body? Alcohol acts in many ways like a pickling agent. From a chemical point of view, it's a cousin to formaldehyde, the preservative agent for cadavers. But instead of stopping bacteria from decomposing a dead body, alcohol stops cells from functioning properly in a live one.

The most dramatic medical effect of alcohol, short of the awful results of mixing teens, booze and automobiles, is alcohol withdrawal. Sixteen-year-old Viola's dad, Miguel, is a case in point. Viola was quiet, gentle and depressed. Her dad was an unemployed carpenter whose union long ago stopped calling him for jobs because of his use of alcohol. Viola's most recent nightmare began when she was awakened by Miguel screaming downstairs. Then the voice of her alarmed mother joined in.

"The Devil is here! He's coming to get me!" Miguel screamed.

"There is no Devil, Miguel. Get back to bed," her mother pleaded.

"I see him. There are three of them!" Miguel raced to the bedroom and seized a .38 caliber handgun. Viola heard footsteps and then the front door open and slam shut. Her mother had fled. "You bastards!" he screamed and fired the gun through the living room window. "Aaaah!" he screamed. "Get off me! Get off!" He was thrashing around on the floor and then suddenly seemed calm.

Viola threw on a bathrobe and crept down the stairs. As she got to the last step, her father bolted upright, his eyes wide as if he were being choked, sweat forming on his forehead and body trembling as if wracked with electric current. He attempted to direct the shaky gun at Viola and growled, "You Devil! I'm going to kill you!" He stood shaking before her, blocking her escape through the front door. Viola froze. Her father seemed to stretch taller, then he dropped to his knees and vomited. Abruptly, his mind seemed to clear. "Viola," he said weakly. But then he became alarmed and began to pick invisible things from his skin. "Get off! Get them off me! The Devil is covering me with spiders! Spi-" With that he fell to the floor again and began to convulse. A second later his body straightened unnaturally as if struck by one large electrical bolt as his head battered repeatedly against the floor without control. That was Viola's chance to break for the door and safety.

During this episode, Miguel was suffering from the delirium tremens. His family was suffering, too. Alcoholism is a disease not only of the patient, but the family as well. Miguel had used alcohol over a prolonged period. He went into withdrawal when he fell asleep, woke in the middle of the night and had no alcohol in the house. Miguel's symptoms: tremors, sweating, insomnia, agitation, nausea and vomiting, all of which are common ones. Convulsions are less so. Miguel suffered multiple types of frightening hallucinations in the senses of sight, sound and touch. This is classic alcoholic withdrawal.

Less dramatic, perhaps, but more heartbreaking, is the damage alcohol does to the ability to learn and remember. When alcohol is drunk in a large enough dose at one time, it will exert a toxic effect on the brain so that new information can't be learned at that time. The following day, the drinker may have no memory of what went on the night before. This is the proverbial blackout. Far worse is the permanent blackout, commonly called Korsakoff's psychosis. Manny is a longtime drinker I met one night in an emergency room.

"Oh, yes, I've seen you before," the ragged man chattered on excitedly.

"In the bank?"

"That's where it was, in Bozeman." he said with conviction.

"In Denver?" I asked.

"That's right. In Denver. I was cashing a check. I won it at the casino."

"They paid you with a check from the casino?"

"It was a business deal. Under the table. You know."

"I don't."

"You know, like my brother. A military secret."

"You saw me in the convenience store?"

"Convenience store? Yes. That's right. I saw you there."

"What was the name of the store?"

"Oh, don't try to quiz me on that one."

"Where was it, the store?"

"Why, let me see. It was in Missoula."

"Missoula? Not Bozeman?"

"Oh, now, I get your drift. Yes, it was…no…Do you think I could have a drink of water?"

Manny had no ability to remember from one moment to the next. Imagine getting out of bed and not remembering the next thing you were supposed to do that day. Imagine how well you would be able to learn the rudiments of staying sober if you had a disease which prevented any learning at all. This is the condition of those sad, end-stage alcoholic folks wandering the streets of cities incapable of staying sober and barely capable of staying alive.

Kids, even alcoholic ones, don't develop this memory problem until decades of drinking have gone by. On the other hand, a kid only needs a single binge (remember, kids binge first and ask questions later) to reach the point of blacking out memories of what happened under the influence. In the short run, blackouts, hangovers and missed classes make drinking a school buster affecting one college kid in four.

Dementia, a close relative of Korsakoff's disease, affects one in ten alcoholics. One somewhat happy note about alcoholic dementia is that sobriety can arrest and possibly improve this condition. What one sees in the advanced stages of this disease are reduced mental abilities in memory combined with difficulty in speaking, planning, organizing and abstracting. Victims look prematurely aged. Once again, without these mental abilities in place, the victims have no weapons with which to fight relapse into drinking and relapse they do.

Alcohol also induces disorders of anxiety, mood, sleep and sexual function. Alcohol dependent persons can suffer insomnia for years following abstinence, especially a reduction in the most restful stage of sleep.

Besides insomnia, alcohol causes liver disease, which in males results in reduced male hormones and an increase in female ones. The outcome is that male alcoholics suffer breast development and wasting of their testes. The list of other medical problems of alcohol is long. A partial list includes inflammation and destruction of the esophagus and stomach, with pain, vomiting and bleeding; pancreatitis, with a 30 percent mortality rate; and multiple diseases of the liver, including fatty degeneration (in 90 percent of the patients), hepatitis (in 40 percent); and cirrhosis.

The good news is that with abstinence a drinker can recover from fatty degeneration and hepatitis, since the liver is a tough organ that heals itself if given half a chance. That is not the case, unfortunately, with cirrhosis, which affects about 20 percent of all chronic drinkers. That's because cirrhosis starts with inflammation and ends up with scarring. The scars, called fibrosis, do not go away once they are there. The result is a raft of complications including uncontrolled swelling of the abdomen and feet, engorged and bursting veins, bleeding disorders, malnutrition and brain dysfunction. These are all medically treatable and helped with abstinence, but some people die. Consider Frank's last ride.

Frank could not stop drinking ever since his father offered him his first beer when he was twelve. "Today you are a man!" his drunken father laughed. His mother thought the drunken child was cute. Drinking occurred in high school and then in his college fraternity, until he flunked out of school. Then drinking took the place of work in a local tile factory, supermarket, shoe store, warehouse, lumberyard and a series of bars.

When I interviewed Frank the few times we met in the emergency room, he was cheerful and engaging. He could talk to people — the lonely, the bored. For a time, he had found his place in the universe as a bartender. But to take the edge off a long night's work, he turned to the owner's stock night after night, until he lost his job. Still he drank, before the rent, before a meal and finally, in place of meals. He was sick, homeless, unemployable. Cirrhosis had scarred his liver and engorged the veins in his throat. On days when he vomited, he would leave bright red blood in the gutter behind him as he struggled up the busy street to panhandle loose change for another small bottle of wine.

"You know, if you don't stop drinking," the earnest intern warned during his last emergency room visit, "you could bleed to death." Frank had heard this before. He smiled playfully as the transfused blood he was receiving bolstered his strength.

"We all gotta go sometime, Doc. By the way," he said with mischief rising in his blue eyes, "where can a fella get a drink around here?" That was the last time I saw Frank. A few weeks later, in a fit of vomiting, he tore veins in his esophagus and lay on the street in a widening circle of blood. On a gurney en route to the emergency room, his heart fluttered and then stopped.

Death by hemorrhage may be one of the more dramatic ends for the alcoholic, but it is not the only end. Alcohol can poison the heart or nerves in your arms and legs. Strokes can occur in drinkers under the age of fifty three times more frequently. Often unappreciated is that 4 percent of all cancers in males are related to alcohol. Alcohol and tobacco are synergistic, meaning that the damage one causes is accelerated by the other *to a greater extent than either one would cause alone.* The result is an increased incidence of cancer of the mouth and throat. If your kid won't take this for a warning, consider the following.

Problem Drinking's Other Problems: Mental Illness

Sooner or later problem drinkers pick up other problems along the way. These include addiction to other drugs. 18 percent of alcohol abusers are also addicted to amphetamines, cocaine and/or heroin. It's in the face of other drugs that alcohol dissolves an addict's resolve to say no. Suzie, one of my patients, came to the hospital to detox from alcohol and heroin. She was a wisp of a girl, shuddering and clutching her abdomen in pain.

Almost immediately I feared the worst news in her clinical history was not the alcohol and heroin. That was bad enough. But given her history of injecting heroin and needle sharing, I drew an antibody test for hepatitis C. Her screening antibody test was positive, as was a confirmatory test for viral RNA in Suzie's blood for this potentially fatal disease. Suzie was a high school student.

Even without such devastating diseases, alcohol is linked to mood and anxiety disorders. Often a kid will get into using alcohol to excess as a self-medication for anxiety or depression. Stephen Gilman at Harvard and I found an apparent answer to the chicken and egg question of which comes first, alcohol abuse or depression. Our study found that the answer is both. That is, if you're depressed, you're more likely to become a problem drinker. And if you're a big time drinker, you're more likely to end up depressed. Gender is important. Male drinkers tend to drink and then become depressed. Females tend to first become depressed and then drink.

Also important is that alcoholic females have a *tenfold* increase in mania compared to non-drinkers, though my suspicion is that the mania comes first. Alcohol is cheaper and easier to get than medication and many bipolar patients treat themselves with booze, even if the benefit of the treatment lasts only a few hours and brings with it a bundle of trouble.

Alcohol is a classic reliever of anxiety. For many kids it may be the life of the party, but it's often a form of self-medication for social anxiety as well. It depends on the person. Certainly stopping a drinking binge abruptly will result in a flood of anxiety and even panic symptoms. But the numbers speak for themselves. Generalized anxiety is found in a quarter of all patients coming into substance abuse programs and half described some form of anxiety at some point in their lifetimes.

The Sneaky Pete of Dependency: How a Kid Becomes Alcoholic

Another young man I was called on to treat was the shy, bright penny that often seemed lost in the clatter of a large Irish family with a dad who drank steadily every night. Brent tended to play alone. On the first day of kindergarten, he wept in panic when his mother tried to leave him for the morning. The shyness never left him. In high school he was handsome, intelligent and a good basketball player. But when it came to dating, he was reduced to a stammering wreck. Teammates tried to talk to possible dates for him, but he was not dating material, mumbling inanities, staring out the window of the backseat of a car while squeezing himself as far away from his date as the door panel would let him.

All that changed when Brent had his first drink. He felt enthusiastic, confident, witty. Girls began to see him this way as well. Brent was becoming the life of any party to which he was invited. And as his party persona became known more widely, he was invited to more of them. Each time he faced a social gathering, he downed the requisite number of beers to transform into a party animal. It was Janet, a girlfriend at the time, who put her finger on the problem when she asked, "Why do we have to drink beers every time before we go out?"

Brent's pattern of drinking widened in scope as he got older. Each time he faced a job interview, exam or date, he turned to alcohol to ease the dread. But there was a downside. He found after several years that he needed to consume more alcohol to achieve the same calming effect. At twenty-six he came to me for help.

Brent's story is typical of a kid easing his way into alcoholism. It's important to recognize that although Brent progressed from life of the party to "partying" for life, his story was the result of a disease, not a moral failure. Only recently has genetic and other biological evidence emerged to support this forty-year-old theory. What we now know about the development of alcoholism is that it is often a Sneaky Pete Dependency, taking years to emerge. Before then, the proto-alcoholic sees himself as the proverbial "party animal," "weekend warrior," "frat boy," or other label of respectability painted over a suspect activity.

It was only years later, when he was in treatment, that Brent came up with the answer. He needed to be drunk, because he was lonely and being drunk enabled him to be with other people. By the time he was in college, his shyness had intensified. If alcohol had served to take the edge off his anxiety, it had also prevented him from learning the skills he needed to make contact with people and still remain sober. By then he also was drinking to relieve hangovers and numb the pain of the disappointments that are an inevitable part of growing up.

Brent's career in the securities firm he joined had also become affected. He could talk to clients on the phone, but only after drinking. He failed to hold onto the clients he developed. A move to the research department brought him little respite. When he first came to treatment, his marriage was in trouble and he was facing a charge of driving while intoxicated.

I found Brent had insight into where his problem came from. Three of his seven brothers and sisters were alcoholic. There was no indication that his parents had tried to intervene in his teen years. Now, on a new kind of edge, the precipice into alcohol dependence, he would have to do it without their help.

Brent told me with a certain degree of understatement, "Alcohol retarded my social development. You don't learn how to deal with socially difficult situations when you're drunk."

In addition to alcohol dependence, he suffered from a clinical diagnosis of social phobia and major depression. So treatment was directed at each of his problems. For his alcohol problem he attended AA and I prescribed two medications for alcohol dependence. For his social phobia and depression, I prescribed a third. The combination of AA, individual therapy and medications was transforming for him. Brent's anxieties in social situations reduced. He noted he could make small talk at his club, on an elevator or a grocery line for the first time in his life. He enthused somewhat exaggeratedly, "My mental abilities have increased five times!" There was evidence from work, though, that his performance was improving. He changed departments again and began telling me that for the first time in years he was enjoying work.

But in the life of an addict, every silver lining has a cloud. In Brent's case it was his need to stop his medications to "see if I could drink again." Of course he could. But as he told me after these disastrous experiments, "One beer invades my mind and then I can't stop," so common a complaint from the alcoholic that this concept relates to two of the diagnostic criteria for substance dependence by the American Psychiatric Association, that:

1. The substance is often taken in larger amounts or over a longer period than was intended and

2. There is a persistent desire or unsuccessful efforts to cut down or control substance use

One telling detail of Brent's alcohol addiction did not make the psychiatrists' list of criteria. To this day, he dreams of drinking.

In males, we see two types of alcoholic patterns: kids who have wild, unlawful teenage years and who abuse alcohol along with other drugs and kids whose alcoholism may start in adolescence, but only fully appears after the age of twenty-five, like Brent. The second group feels guilt and shame about what drinking does to their lives. The first group frequently does not. For girls, the disease has a later age of appearance, but with more devastating effects, since a girl who starts her drinking career in adolescence may fail to realize how bad things are until she is in her thirties or forties, after two decades of a life battered by booze.

So Where Does Alcoholism Come From?

Theories range from the social to the biological. I can summarize the most important factors in a single word: **SLOGS.** This stands for:

1. **S**ocial pressure.
2. **L**earning.
3. **O**pportunity.
4. **G**enes.
5. **S**elf-medication.

I've already talked about the kinds of pressures kids are under to take chances, behave like stereotyped adults, look macho or sophisticated and alter their consciousness for the sake of the party. Kids learn to drink. We as parents teach them, for better or worse. Genes, as I've mentioned, are also important. Alcohol as self-medication is used often by kids for social phobia, other anxiety disorders or depression.

What about race and ethnicity? The answer is that we don't know about their roles. The problem with existent studies is that they don't always address important factors which may equally explain the finding, such as differences in economic status, language, environment, alcohol and drug availability and access to health care. However, a few findings are worth noting. Asian-Americans, for example, have lower rates of alcoholism. This may be in large part, because half of this population lacks a gene that metabolizes alcohol in the liver. A person without this gene will suffer facial flushing and discomfort after drinking that makes alcohol less than the ideal party drug.

The firewater theory, the notion that Native Americans are at higher risk for alcohol because they are more sensitive to the effects of alcohol, is false. If anything, Native Americans may be less sensitive to booze, but at greater risk when they move from rural to urban centers.

The rates of alcohol dependence among African-Americans are similar to whites, but the death rates of black drinkers from alcohol-related causes are two and one-half times higher than whites. Why should African-Americans have more cirrhosis and alcohol-related homicide? My guess is that these deaths are tied to economic disadvantage, because poverty closes many doors to treatment. There is one great lesson in all the findings. That is, what happens in a kid's environment is key to whether he or she develops alcoholism, regardless of race. In other words, alcoholism is an equal opportunity employer. The word "employer" is accurate. Being a dependent drunk is a job that eventually replaces all the other jobs of life.

How to Tell If Your Child Is an Alcoholic

Does your child drink? Ask her. This is a test of trust between parent and child. Does your child's breath smell from liquor when he comes home from a party? Is he throwing up often or smelling like he has? Are you getting hints from the local police department late at night? Evidence your kid has been drinking is not evidence she is alcohol dependent. Far more likely, it's a little experimentation. Not parent approved, but experimentation nonetheless.

More worrisome are repeated episodes of drunkenness. These, too, may occur in kids who are not in other kinds of trouble. This, however, signals potential dangers. Alcohol remains a major factor in auto accidents, date rape, homicides and suicides. These are teenage landmines even in the absence of a full-blown alcohol addiction. Consider the story of Craig.

Over six feet tall and 191 lbs., Craig was starting defensive tackle of the local high school football team in his senior year. His use of drugs was minimal — a toke or two of marijuana at a party when it was available. But alcohol was another story. Wine coolers led to vodka tonics which led to Jell-O shots. These led to half of the seniors on the team stealing a few chickens from a local farm the night before the game with an important rival and attempting to kick the birds to death in a playground. Craig and others ran when they saw the flashers of the oncoming patrol car. However, the playground had high fences. The police caught them there and arrested the boys at the entrance. Craig, an otherwise decent kid, had allowed alcohol to turn him into something of a monster. This is not alcohol dependence, but abuse. That the judge mandated him to attend alcohol education classes is a sign of an enlightened judicial program.

Other warning signs of alcohol abuse include repeated use of booze resulting in failure to fulfill major obligations at work, school or home; repeated use in physically hazardous situations; repeated alcohol-related legal problems or continued use of alcohol despite recurring alcohol-related problems. Just *one* of the events signals that alcohol is getting a kid into trouble.

A quantum jump in trouble faces the kids who become alcohol dependent. These individuals are less likely to reveal themselves in adolescence, which means that interventions should occur with signs of early abuse, the initial point in a kid's natural history of using drugs and alcohol. Typical is Sharkey, whose history of drinking excessively as a kid led to more serious problems.

Sharkey was trouble in kindergarten. He was violent towards other kids, could not keep his seat for any period of time and often could not understand spoken instructions. The rest of his remaining nine grades of education were little better. He was well-known to the local police. By the age of twelve, he had been charged with assault, assault and battery, breaking and entering, as well as assault with a deadly weapon.

Despite a habit to punch out people who looked twice at him, he was only five feet seven inches tall and a scrawny 143 pounds, which he often hid behind a dark overcoat. In his teen years he took drugs and then prowled the streets for people to beat up.

Sharkey boasted of his history.

"I was great," he told the emergency room psychiatrist. "We'd get high on a six pack and some 'ludes and go lookin' for a faggot to beat on." The interviewer was trying to balance her professional neutrality while the patient was regaling her with his accomplishments.

"What if you couldn't find any homosexuals to beat up?"

"Oh, then we'd find other kids in our neighborhood and have, you know, a gang bang. The 'ludes made it great. You know how you usually feel when you punch someone in the mouth? I guess you don't...."

"Wasn't it painful? Punching people that way?"

"Painful to them, maybe. You try to make 'em bleed. That was the best," he enthused. "Only thing you might get was a few cuts on your knuckles. But with the booze you never felt a thing."

"Did you punch gays in the mouth?"

"Oh, yeah, all the time," Sharkey said with feelings that were part pride and part yearning for his prey.

"Is that how you got AIDS? From their blood? You know, in the cuts on your knuckles?"

Sharkey stopped for a moment. "Nah. Not that. It was from all the sex. If you play, you gotta pay."

The playing to which Sharkey alluded included a career of alcohol use which resulted in needing increasing amounts in order to feel the same effect (tolerance); getting sick the next morning after an alcohol binge (withdrawal); continuing use of alcohol and drugs despite knowledge that it was causing him medical problems. He had tried after a few brief jail sentences to clean up, but could not stay sober for more than a week or so. Now drugging and drinking had replaced any hope of family, work and a stable home as he wandered down a spiraling path of alcohol dependence and AIDS.

Treatment? Yes!

When your child has broadcast to you any one of the signals that alcohol or drugs are a problem, act! This is Heads-up Parenting. Don't wait for a kid to progress from alcohol abuse to alcohol dependence to polydrug dependence. The earlier the intervention, the better the result. Treatment works.

However, getting kids to accept treatment may be difficult. First, kids are slow to recognize a problem, since it's all rock and roll to them. Kicking and screaming are not unheard of when kids are brought in for treatment. Second, alcohol or drugs are oftentimes not the only issue. The young person with these problems may have special needs, like being pregnant or HIV positive. He may be remanded to treatment by the court. There may be depression, mania, psychosis or other forms of drug abuse with which to deal. There may be turmoil in the family or problems with school. Because our children are our dependents, kids depend on their parents and clinicians to deal with more problems than other adults do. Third, relapse in kids occurs as it does in adults. The good news is that kids relapse less often from ingrained patterns of chemical addiction and more often because of a complex interplay of factors in the child's personality, values and environment. So the goal of treatment is not perfection, but the maximal number of alcohol- and drug-free days. How do we get there?

Talk to your pediatrician and ask if she has recommendations about dealing with a kid using alcohol. The pediatrician may refer you to a competent community resource if she feels under-trained in handling drug abuse problems. Different kids bring different problems. Not all programs fit all kids. Here are a few guidelines:

If a kid has had a single episode of alcohol abuse, you may not need an expert. Consistent limit setting by the parents may accomplish the goal. *Consistent* is the keyword. A united front by two parents is more than twice as effective as two differing fronts. The Volvo Company was one of the first automakers to realize that in every marriage, one partner likes the front seat warm and the other likes it cool. So they put *two* temperature controls in the front seats. It's human nature for two people to see things differently. Two parents struggling with a kid's drug use are bound to disagree. Mr. and Mrs. Barkley showed these differences.

The Barkleys were churchgoers. He was an accountant. She was a homemaker active in the PTA and had a small business selling household products from home. The father was a hawk when it came to drugs.

"I told him, 'Damn it, you are NOT allowed to drink alcohol under any circumstance until you are the age of twenty-one. Period!"

Mrs. Barkley was a dove. "Don," she told her husband, "It's a little beer. What harm will it do? He can drink under supervision on the weekend."

"You know my feelings about that, Emma. I don't want the kid drinking at all. That's all there is to it!"

"If he doesn't do it at home, do you want him to do it out on the street? Why are you going off your rocker over a single beer?"

This was hardly the road to a united front. Even though this conversation took place while their son, Reggie, was out, it was impossible for the boy to miss the differences of opinion between his parents and to exploit them by using his mother's values against his father's. What Mr. and Mrs. Barkley needed to do and soon, was to work out an agreement between themselves regarding what would and wouldn't be acceptable behavior for Reggie. A family therapist helped with this job.

James, another kid whose family became alarmed about his drinking, found his way to a counselor after washing out of treatment in two previous tries. His new therapist had an offbeat approach that appealed to James. This time James talked. He began to discover feelings that had been buried under mountains of indifference and bravado.

"I'm drinking a lot more than my mom and dad know. You're not gonna tell them?" he asked anxiously.

"No, only in matters of life and death would I do that. Was this a matter of life and death?" the therapist asked.

"Not really."

"That doesn't sound like an absolute 'no.' What do you mean, 'Not really'?"

"It was kind of stupid. We were drunk and you know that old train trestle off Mill Street?"

"Yes?"

"We were drinkin' beer and just tryin' throw each other off the trestle."

"Oh, I get it. You were drunk and trying to kill each other?"

"No, not kill each other. We weren't too drunk."

"Did anyone get hurt?"

"One guy hit his shoulder on a rock. I guess the water wasn't so deep."

James's realization that he was risking his life by using alcohol led to a final insight in his treatment, the fate of his older brother, Tom. The family had watched in helpless horror as Tom, a shining light for James, had slipped away from their reach into a tide of alcohol abuse. Tom's death at twenty from a motorcycle accident was an alcohol fatality from which the family felt it would never recover. They never talked about their older son's death. It was a taboo. It was a taboo in James's therapy, too, until one day the therapist decided it was time to approach the subject.

"You don't talk much about your brother Tom."

"No. He's dead and gone."

"You said he died in an accident."

"Yeah?"

"And he was drinking."

"What's your point?"

"Do you think there's any parallel between his use of alcohol and your own?" the therapist asked softly.

"Yeah. I'm alive and he's not. How about that?"

James's bravado did not last long. James knew his therapist was telling him he was on the same path as his brother and if he didn't change, he could die as well. Shortly afterwards, James asked for and was referred to a therapy group for teen drinkers in a local church. In an uncommon event in the treatment histories of teenagers, James made the decision that in the future he would simply refuse to drink alcohol. A follow-up five years later found him in graduate school, still abstinent.

Leaderless self-help groups, effective with adults, are not suggested for teens. Unsupervised group therapy among teens brings to mind *Lord of the Flies*. Neither is supervised wilderness trips recommended. There is no evidence that climbing on a rope over a chasm, as attractive as that may be to certain kids, cures alcoholism. Rather, thoughtful group therapy by experienced leaders over time is the best choice. Professional psychiatric care is needed for kids with added burdens of mood disorders or psychosis.

Short-term hospitalizations are helpful when a kid has to clean up from alcohol and drugs. (More about this process is in chapter 18). I have found two medications useful for fighting different aspects of alcohol dependence: Revia and Antabuse. While their use in kids is rare, they should be kept in mind when they fit the clinical problem. Revia is a newcomer to our armamentarium. Recent studies show that it reduces a drinker's craving for alcohol. Antabuse is an old tool. Antabuse does nothing unless you drink alcohol while on it. Then it makes you sick. The sickness comes in the form of vomiting breakfast, lunch and dinner all at the same time. For selected young people, Antabuse works. It adds new meaning to a kid saying, "I can't drink. I'm on medication."

Dealing with an addiction like alcohol dependence is like trying to save yourself as you tumble off a cliff. You can grab onto a root or branch with one finger or as many fingers as you can get around it. The best strategy is not a single approach, but multiple ones. It's hard, but this methodology can save your child's life. Finally, in the midst of outrageous behavior by the alcohol abusing kid, don't forget that with sobriety almost always comes a better person and the hope of a better life.

Take-Home Lesson #8

1) Set consistent limits at the first occurrence of alcohol consumption.
2) There is no such thing as "controlled drinking" by teenagers.
3) Ban the use of alcohol as a rite of passage.
4) Reject the drinking, not the child.
5) Treat the alcohol addicted kid with multiple approaches at the same time.

Chapter 9

Acid: The Good, the Bad and the Permanent

A young, studious-looking man sat before me in the psychiatric emergency department of a large Boston hospital. He appeared calm and thoughtful. He had asked to speak with a psychiatrist, but would not say why. Now he said he wanted to ask me a few questions about consciousness.

"I'm writing a book about the subject," he explained.

"Tell me about it," I said pensively. People don't usually talk to me about "consciousness" in an emergency room unless it's preceded by "clouded," "semi" or "un." But the man was in a high-powered academic town. Harvard and Massachusetts Institute of Technology are a stone's throw across the Charles River. Maybe he's a graduate student, I speculated.

"The first chapter is a review of the world's literature."

Maybe he *is* writing a book on consciousness, I mused. "What's in the second chapter?"

"A discussion of the major thinkers in the field, where they agree, the controversies."

I was beginning to be impressed. He went on.

"And then the major thesis, the antithesis and the synthesis."

A little bit of Hegel, I thought, but as he rambled on and on with his description, I began getting lost. As he continued talking, I realized that this "book" was leaving me completely in the dark.

"I'm sorry, but I don't understand what you're talking about," I broke in. "What exactly is your thesis about consciousness?"

He looked at me with a mixture of pity and disdain. "Of course you don't understand. Don't you realize I am not from this planet."

And then I did understand. As we spoke further, he told me that he had once been on planet earth, but that was before he began using LSD. It was after those trips that his life of delusions began.

Probably no drug touched the imagination of psychiatrists more than the discovery of lysergic acid diethylamide, known to both the Drug Enforcement Agency and street users as LSD or simply "acid." LSD comes from a bit of creative chemistry with a class of drugs, ergotamines, that is ancient. These drugs, when eaten in large quantities, make your arms and legs fall off. For real. Ergotamines are formed by a fungus that grows in rye flour. Off and on in medieval Europe, people would eat rye bread poisoned with ergot and die. The survivors called the poisoning St. Anthony's Fire. Forty thousand people died this way in 944 AD.

But LSD has no such effects. When Albert Hofmann first accidentally ate LSD contaminated food, he went on history's first bona fide head trip. Not knowing what had caused this mind-bending ride, but knowing he had come back down with a soft landing, he thought it was something he ate. So he went back to the lab and tasted every new compound on the shelf. He took meticulous notes to define his reaction to each drug tasted.

When Hofmann got to LSD, his note taking became uncommonly brief. It reads, "4/29/43 16:30 Solution of diethylamide tartrate orally = 0.25mg. Taken diluted with 10cc water. Tasteless. 17:00 Beginning dizziness, feeling of anxiety, visual distortions, symptoms of paralysis, desire to laugh." There the note taking stopped.

However, millions of others followed this reluctant Pied Piper into the next century, tripping their ways to serenity, insight or lasting nightmares.

Good and Bad Trip

Marina was the valedictorian of her high school class, summa cum laude in neuroscience at an Ivy League university and a star in graduate school. She married another student, Grigor, whose career was less luminous and who was content to follow her from post to post as she advanced through academia. On the edge of a Southwestern canyon one morning, Marina decided to examine her inner life in a way that her slowly moving psychotherapy could not. She swallowed 100 micrograms of crystalline LSD, also known as windowpane.

She had read *The Doors of Perception* by Aldous Huxley and Albert Hofmann's classic on acid, *LSD, My Problem Child*. Marina's Ph.D. thesis was based on her research into the very neuroreceptors that acid was known to affect. She was not naïve about drugs. In graduate school she had smoked dope occasionally. Once, she had been so intoxicated on strong stuff, she had been unable to pipette solutions the next day. Knowing herself to be of sound mind and body, she was as prepared as anyone could be for the adventure. But, as she would say afterwards, "It wasn't like reading the funny pages."

The acid hit her hard. Her mind flowed with unbidden emotions from anxiety to joy to hurt and grief. Images rose up before her, taking their initial shapes from the rocks and cacti around her, but stretching and shrinking into faces, colors and indefinable globs. Clouds raced across the sky as if driven by invisible charioteers. She later could not remember if sounds became pictures or vice versa. Emotions heaped up as she thought of the people in her life. Her career appeared to fall away from her as so much discarded pieces of glassware, receding before her gaze in colored winds which seemed to blow them away, visible, swirling, but smaller and smaller and then but a memory.

By late afternoon, Marina's flight into fancy began to drift downward. She felt waves of paranoia, fearing the police were watching her in the canyon. Then came a cleansing sense of well-being and mental clarity as if for the first time in years she felt like her life once again had important direction. The following morning her husband asked her how her first trip had been.

"Grigor, it's hard to explain," she started. "I think I want a divorce."

Although she eventually did divorce her husband, she credited the experience with helping her see something in her life she was incapable of seeing without the help of the drug. As Huxley had deemed in *The Doors of Perception,* passing through those chemically constructed doors changed her life forever. And, she believed, she was better off for it.

Reports such as Marina's, to say nothing of those by eminent teachers at famous universities, unleashed a flood of claims that LSD could treat many of the cruelest psychiatric illnesses, including alcoholism, schizophrenia and infantile autism. These claims were based on research that was conceived and conducted more out of enthusiasm than methodological care. The result is that to date none of these claims appears credible.

Other claims appear to be on even shakier ground. Does LSD cure allergies to cats? Is it a guide for the perplexed? Does it make you more creative? There's no real evidence for these beyond muddy case reports. Ideas like these are devilishly hard to prove, even when they appear to be intuitively correct. Nevertheless, sometimes the mud of case reports can lead to more solid conclusions. Some patients have reported LSD use in their development and then moved on to better ways of growing.

Like others, Jana was an LSD experimenter. She was a young, bright woman in search of herself through chemicals. She had gone through a decade of dope and acid and come through intact. Her career had taken off as a computer specialist. She had met and fallen in love with a caring partner. Unlike many of her friends in those years, she saw herself as coming through her decade of drug experimentation unscathed. I asked her how she did it, when she knew a number of people who didn't fare so well.

"You asked about the difference between people who came away from LSD experiences relatively undamaged or otherwise poetic, metaphorical and in love with life and those who came away very damaged, in apparent chaotic states of consciousness. I remember clearly the visual image of new thought pathways being created when I tripped, sort of like rolling a ball through the sand, creating a groove that it was easier to go down next time round the course. Trouble was, not all of these grooves were good ones, and one had to exercise more discipline (effectively deepening other grooves) to keep from returning to the bad ones. In fact, most of the people I know who have been damaged as a result of their LSD experiences just got stuck in one of those pathways that originally happened on a trip and never really even saw that's what had happened to them. The other 'problem area' was for people who did not have enough mental elasticity. Their worlds were very tightly circumscribed and the revelation that things were not as they had self-constructed them was very difficult and destabilizing for them... Once again my answer comes back to will, mental elasticity and a certain degree of luck. Recognizing that I was falling into some of those bad grooves, I worked very hard to avoid them and not go back there. Finding myself in a groove that felt good, right and clear, I worked very hard (and, I suppose to this day continue to work hard) nurturing those patterns."

What about those who came away damaged? What kind of damage are we talking about?

The Bad Trip

Though Huxley said that you would not be the same as you had been once you came back through the "doors of perception," he didn't guarantee that you'd be better off. That was the problem with Tino, who one night was driving his SUV on a four lane interstate highway.

Like Marina, he had dropped about 100 micrograms of crystalline acid, but there the similarity of his experience ends. His girlfriend, Mercedes, was on the seat beside him, lighting a joint and bouncing to the music. For Tino, the sounds of the music from the radio began to get slower and get louder. Shadowy people were waving to him from the sides of the road. The headlights of passing cars appeared fascinating, then ominous. Long colored streaks were left in place as the cars and trucks drove past him.

Mercedes changed the dial to a station playing Latino music. The colored streaks began to look bizarre. Tino thought there were faces in them. His head was pulsing with the music. His heart seemed to beat in time, faster and faster. He wanted to close his eyes. He had trouble breathing. Beads of sweat popped out on his forehead. The words from the radio were speaking to him, for him, about him. They were his words, his ideas on the radio. They were

Mercedes' words. She was calling his name. He turned to her. But she was gone. In her place was a giant spider groping towards him. He screamed. He kicked at the spider with his foot, pressing himself to the door. As he did, he heard the voice of Mercedes yell his name as his car swerved off the highway and rolled.

Tino survived to tell me the tale. However, Tino did not leave the experience without wounds. Indeed, they have lasted a lifetime and include panic attacks as well as a shaken, self-doubting soul. Alcohol dependence followed as he tried in vain to control the panicked feelings with booze. The panic attacks are often treatable with medication, but in Tino's case it has not been a good idea to give him drugs of the benzodiazepine class, an ordinarily excellent treatment for panic disorder, since abusing one drug can result in abusing all abusable drugs. And the benzodiazepines (Valium, Ativan, Xanax, Klonopin, among others) may be misused and are abusable. *Abusable* is the operative word here. It would be cruel and self-defeating to withhold other types of anti-panic medication from drug abusers with panic attacks. Self-defeating, because without treatment the drug abuser would be more inclined to return to self-medication and relapse. Yet, Tino did better than another patient I had, Eddie, who had irreversible wounds.

Eddie was popular, even loved, by his classmates at a small western college. A biology student with a large romantic streak, his favorite kind of date was to bring a girl to an abandoned granite quarry, lie on a blanket, drop acid and be entertained by the dancing stars. One night the dancing stars invited him to join in. Madeline on the blanket giggled quietly and she watched her cigarette forming designs in the air.

"I am the one!" his voice echoed triumphantly against the faces of granite, as Madeline sought the meaning in cigarette smoke. "I am at one, at one with the moon!" he enthused, gliding on his feet. He was dancing about the edge of the quarry, his head tossed back to drink in the universe. The stars and Eddie were choreographing one another. "I can touch them," he said. He leapt to touch them; he leapt again. The quarry fell silent. After a minute Madeline realized Eddie was no longer on the mossy edge. He was unconscious and paralyzed lying on a ledge in bushes twenty feet below.

The Permanent Trip

Acid can cause more than temporary losses of good judgment. Because it has especially powerful effects on vision, about 40 percent of kids who try the drug describe lingering visual aftereffects. For most, these so-called "flashbacks" spontaneously disappear in a matter of months to years. But for some, this problem, hallucinogen persisting perception disorder (HPPD), can last their lifetimes. Gloria, another young woman I saw, had this continuing problem.

Gloria was a wild kid, into alcohol at eleven, pot at twelve and acid from ages thirteen to fifteen. The first two were "O.K." to her way of thinking, but LSD was her drug of choice. She didn't trip more than a half dozen times, though, when she first began to notice she could see the trailing images of her hand as she moved it in front of her face. Certain colors which she remembered from previous trips, like the clashing purples of the Dunkin' Donuts logo, could make her feel as if she were tripping again when she saw them straight. Her friends told her she was just getting "free trips" and should enjoy them.

She tried to, but the high came more often, lasted longer and was less fun than before. Then one evening she smoked a joint with friends, passed on the acid, but felt as if she was on acid all over again. The next morning, she was still high. The trails of her hands were brighter. She looked at the blank television and looked away. There was another image of the television looking at her on the blank wall. Outdoors trees looked as if their leaves were bending down ominously at her. Gloria jumped, thinking she saw a cat beside her. These symptoms have continued for the last thirty years.

HPPD is an especially troublesome after-effect of LSD. What we think happens in HPPD is that certain vulnerable people — and we can't tell who they are in advance — suffer permanent changes in brain function after LSD, especially in the nerve cells that ordinarily help the brain filter out extraneous visual input. With these cells out of commission, a little stimulation goes a long way, creating a broad array of visual and emotional sensations which are extremely difficult to treat.

The good news here is that HPPD will not kill you. The visual disturbances can be annoying and even impairing. However, other psychiatric illnesses that go along with HPPD are the critical ones to watch for—alcoholism, mood, anxiety and psychotic disorders— *each of which can and should be, treated.* The symptoms of HPPD may at times be controlled with certain medications, including clonidine, naltrexone, sertraline and the benzodiazepines, but the evidence for this is muddy.

Clinically, a kid with HPPD does best by avoiding abusable drugs and alcohol, especially pot, since pot can precipitate or worsen HPPD in a quantum jump in a single night. The other important dimension in its treatment is often undervalued — psychotherapy. Kids with HPPD are usually demoralized into thinking that their lives are over, because they see themselves as damaged goods. Nothing is farther from the truth, but try convincing a kid with HPPD of that. Nevertheless, I have seen HPPD patients grow up and become successful parents, doctors, psychologists, bankers and computer wizards leading completely normal lives.

The other complication from acid is psychosis. One kid in five with HPPD will also develop psychosis. This illness, too, is treatable, but treatment can be slow, complicated, frustrating and ineffective. The victories, however, when they come, are all the sweeter for the effort.

One patient who struggled with this problem was Sam. In the eleventh grade Sam was a starting member of his high school soccer team, popular with both girls and boys despite a reputation for shyness. He was a member of the ecology club. He, unfortunately, read with excitement Timothy Leary's call to tune in, turn on and drop out. He was drawn to the Grateful Dead. He attended one of their concerts. A deadhead offered him a hit of acid for five dollars. He wondered why he couldn't tune in, turn on and still go to college. Turning on was fun. Tripping during Dead concerts was the most wonderful feeling in his life. If the acid wasn't strong enough, adding alcohol would help.

After his third concert, Sam began to feel that something was wrong. Back in school he sat in class with his eyes fixed at a place somewhere between his desk and the window. He noticed flashes of color shooting like sheet lightning across the room. The walls of the classroom appeared to be breathing. Outdoors, the air looked like billions of vibrating colored dots.

"What?" he called out softly in class one day.

"Sam?" the teacher asked. "Did you want to say something?"

"N-no," Sam muttered in confusion.

Sam had heard his first hallucination. At their best, his hallucinations entertained him with music. At their worst they drove him to flee from his class and, finally, hide from the brightly lit outdoors he had loved so well. He stopped eating. He became pale, fearful and bizarre. At home when watching television at night, he suddenly would get up and turn it off.

"They were talking about me on television. They said I was destroying Earth," he later told me. To counter the voices, Sam argued with them and shrieked in his room. His parents were frightened and confused. This was not their sweet boy.

"I'm *not* the polluter, man!" he shouted with rising apprehension. "People are polluters...I'm not a person... I'm a seal...a baby seal." At this point Sam was too afraid to go to school. In desperation his parents called a psychiatrist. The earliest appointment they could arrange was three weeks away. Eight days later Sam attempted to drown himself in the bathroom toilet. "To be in the sea, to be with the baby seals," he muttered as he looked away from me in the emergency room. Hair wet and tangled, he half-looked like the hunted animal he believed he was.

"I couldn't think, things seemed so weird. I heard voices in class calling my name," he told me later after he had been admitted to the psychiatric unit. "The voice first came once in a while, then every day, then every minute...I hear them now..." he admitted with his gaze fixed to the floor.

"What does the voice say to you?" I asked.

"My name. They're talking about me."

"Yes?"

"They say I'm a faggot...they want to kill me."

What Sam's family and Sam had to do in the next month was among the hardest things they ever faced together. Sam's father, a local minister and his mother, an officer in the church, were committed to Sam's recovery at each step. He struggled with his voices. Medications and therapy helped, but there were side effects. At one point Sam claimed a previous medication worked for the voices, but "It destroyed my will to live."

To make things harder, Sam struggled with sobriety, turning at times to binging with booze to "stop the voices" and help him regain for a few moments the pleasure that seemed to have drained out of his life with his illness. Then, following a relapse, he attended Alcoholics Anonymous. He needed months of empirical trials of medications to find the right combination to stop Sam's voices decisively and fend off the ever-present threat of depression and suicide. Finally, both he and his family needed ongoing therapy after discharge to help them negotiate each of the twists and turns in helping Sam recover.

Not every physician can treat every patient. This is certainly the case with psychosis, the treatment of which is as much an art form as a science. Sam's family had the tenacity to search out a doctor who had the critical combination of empathy and experience to do her job. Notice I didn't say *the* job, because the input of Sam's family and Sam's own commitment to get well were as powerful as any medication he took.

Not all post-drug psychoses are like Sam's. At times the sneaky onset of the illness after acid use makes drawing a firm connecting line from drug use to psychotic break less certain. But the patient who becomes acutely psychotic immediately after taking a hallucinogen like LSD, hearing and seeing things that aren't there or believing outlandish ideas — delusions — that simply are not true, leaves little to the imagination regarding their cause.

Thus, Helen, a college student who believed the Central Intelligence Agency was plotting to assassinate her during an acid trip and that she was the Queen of Staten Island, continued to hold this delusion for five days after using the drug. Her mood, it's important to know, was elevated and excitable. She laughed and joked a great deal even as she faced assassination. This suggested that the drug had induced a manic episode. Hospitalization followed a dinner at a four star restaurant where she refused the $93 check, claiming the meal was her right of royalty. In the hospital, treating her with lithium along with an anti-psychotic drug was decisive. She left the hospital after five days, mentally clear and somewhat embarrassed. Less fortunate was Steven, gifted with scientific curiosity, who'd taken thirty plus trips on acid at the age of fourteen. In Steven's case, his grandiosity and visual hallucinations never fully yielded to treatment.

Free without Frequent Flyer Miles

I am often asked how many trips a kid needs to develop panic disorder, alcoholism, depression, psychosis or HPPD following LSD. The answer is one. One trip. Many young people find that hard to believe, but it's the truth. The reason is that not everyone reacts to the drug in the same way. One major factor in a person getting into trouble from LSD may be a genetic vulnerability to its long-term effects. Since we can't predict who is going to be unlucky enough to develop a chronic reaction, I tell kids that using LSD is playing Russian Roulette, but with chemicals instead of bullets.

Another problem for users of LSD is suicide. The risk of suicide in kids is low, but increased by the presence of depression, a prior suicide attempt and, yes, drug abuse. Suicidal thinking affects about one-quarter of all teenaged girls at one time or another. What should a parent do about it? As a parent you are not likely to be running a mental hospital or emergency room (though there may be days when you think you are). That means you should leave the diagnosis of suicidal risk to mental health professionals. The slightest whiff of a suicidal danger means you must take your child to the appropriate psychiatric or psychological service. Talk of suicide is nothing to take lightly.

Survival Tips for Parents of Psychotic Kids

The long-term consequences of LSD and similar hallucinogens are illnesses like psychosis and depression, which can wear out families as well as victims over a period of years. To help you cope in this difficult time, here are a few of the principles I have gleaned over the years in working with my patients and their families.

1. Find a competent, knowledgeable mental health professional with whom your child and you are comfortable. Seeing the same one over years is best. There is nothing more helpful than a solid working relationship with a psychiatrist or other mental health professional over the long haul. One who knows each member of your family and is a good listener. One who gives you his or her home phone, not just the number of an answering service. One who returns phone calls promptly and instills trust, confidence and hope.

2.   When you cannot find the perfect professional (since there is no such person on the planet), find someone nearly as good or failing that, a few people with complementary skills (e.g., a psychopharmacologist and a psychotherapist) who come close to your standards. Make sure they talk to each other. A good rule is that the fewer people involved in care, the more unified the treatment plan.

3.   Recognize the importance of medications in the treatment of many post-LSD disorders. These include antipsychotic, mood stabilizer, anti-anxiety and anti-depressant medications. Give them exactly as prescribed, communicate benefits and side effects to the psychiatrist often. Be patient. They can take weeks and months to work. Treatment with medications is rational, but empirical. You have to go slowly, make careful observations and then adjustments.

4.   If you are a cigarette smoker, quit and get your kid to quit smoking. Besides reducing your own and his chances of multiple forms of vascular disease and cancer, you will improve the effects of psychiatric medications on the child and reduce his depression.

5.   Eat better and feed your child better, more nutritional food. One point of good nutrition in mental illness is to provide protein containing the essential amino acids tryptophan and tyrosine, which make serotonin and norepinephrine. The latter are neurotransmitters critical for recovery from depression, among other disorders. No, do not feed your kid dietary supplements. Chicken and fish are best, not megavitamins.

6.   Use psychiatric hospitals for your child only when you must—to prevent suicide, homicide and to control unbearable symptoms. Remember what I call the Four-fold Way for the treatment of psychosis: 1) reduce hospital stays in number and length, 2) reduce the burden of symptoms, 3) increase employment and 4) increase socialization.

7.   Use additional mental health professionals when their unique services are needed. These may include case managers, drug abuse counselors and sponsors, social workers and occupational therapists. But too many cooks spoil the treatment. So coordinate all treatments for your son or daughter through your primary mental health professional.

8.   Do everything you can to help your child. You can provide emotional and financial support. You can set limits. You can avoid

enabling further drug abuse.

9.   If he is driving you and the rest of your family crazy, stop doing everything for your child. It does no good for one sick person in the family to make everyone else sick. There is a place for ostracism in the care of the mentally ill. Your child may need more than you can give. Living at home may be making him sicker. For these cases we have community residences, halfway houses and special schools.

10. Do not under any circumstance give up hope. Never, ever. Miracles happen.

Let me share one. My patient Walter was in a state hospital. He had been there for thirteen years following a spate of acid trips that left him overwhelmed. He had voices in his head that spoke continuously and fixed fears that he was the object of possession by aliens. His speech was a jumble of allusions to the FBI, KGB and "zeebies." He seemed incapable of normal conversation.

Before his life as a mental patient, Walter had been alternatively a street kid, acid dealer and computer technician. Despite his mental illness he had shown a mechanical gift, taking apart the ward's phone one day with a paper clip (to protect us from being wiretapped). Every class of antipsychotic drug available had been tried on him over his thirteen years, but the voices and delusions never left him. It was with no great expectations that I started him on a course of a new medication, clozapine. This was not a drug for all patients. First, it didn't appear to help everyone. Second, it can drop a person's white blood count to dangerous levels and requires weekly blood tests. To my surprise, Walter tolerated the medication well. By the third day he told me, "You know, Doc, the voices aren't as loud as they once were." This was remarkable on two counts. His hallucinations were decreasing and he was beginning to speak in whole sentences for the first time since I had known him. Two weeks after he started the new medication, I was able to have the following coherent conversation with him.

"Any voices?"

"No, they're going away."

" When did you last hear them?"

"I dunno. Maybe a week ago."

"How about alien possession? You've been worried about that, too."

"No, I don't think that's happening anymore."

"Do you have any idea what you'd do if you got well enough to leave the hospital?"

"I'd probably go out for a month or so and hear voices again and come back," he said with a sad laugh.

"You know, your voices and delusions are going away. What if they stayed away?"

"That'd be...that'd be good. Then," he said, raising his hand to grasp a second chance at life, "I think I'd try to learn more about computers."

And so he did.

Remember, even if you have a son or daughter who, like Walter, has been suffering very serious effects of the drugs he or she ahs been taking for a very long time, there is still hope. One day, perhaps tomorrow or years from now, there may be an effective treatment for the disease which has been destroying not only his or her life, but your own. Keep searching for answers.

Take-Home Lesson #9

1) Tripping on acid is playing Russian roulette using chemicals instead of bullets.
2) LSD can cause lifelong visual hallucinations and psychosis in the unlucky kid even after one or two trips.
3) Find a competent, caring mental health professional(s).
4) Psychiatry has tools to treat the most dangerous complications of hallucinogens.
5) Medication may be needed to treat post-LSD disorders.
6) If your child talks of suicide, get help fast.
7) Never give up hope. Ever.

Chapter 10

Ecstasy: The Dark Side

The chemical name is 3,4-methylenedioxymethamphetamine, abbreviated to MDMA. Its street name is what users optimistically call Ecstasy or simply E. It was first invented by the Merck Company in 1914 and sold as a diet pill. Because of its ability to cause euphoria and stimulate mental insights, a few mental health professionals have promoted it as a tool for psychotherapy. However, the most widespread use is recreational and in young people the numbers are growing.

Stupid Tricks Done by Young People on Ecstasy

Some of the most lethal stupid tricks by young people are done on the drug Ecstasy. A good bet is car surfing. First you get high on E. Then you balance yourself on the roof of a car while your friend, also high on E, drives. You pretend you're on a surfboard. Your friend pretends he's still on planet Earth. Needless to say, kids die doing this one.

A less dangerous, more widespread trick is raving. This occurs when a huge number of kids, maybe even 1,000, pack themselves into an airless warehouse, drop E and dance until the sun comes up. The sophisticated clubs where raves take place park ambulances in the back to cart away the casualties. Young people can die at this one, too, as did a medical student at the club Twilo in New York in 2003. More on raves later.

Who Uses E?

Mostly kids, teenagers and young adults in their twenties. From 1999 through 2000, numbers were up sharply in high schoolers. Among eighth graders, use within the preceding twelve months was up from 1.7 to 3.1 percent. Among twelfth graders, use was up from 5.6 to 8.2 percent. Ecstasy is used by American teens more than cocaine.

Only a third of twelfth graders see "great risk" in using Ecstasy. Among college kids, Ecstasy use rose from 0.5 percent in 1994 to 5.5 percent in 1999. This rise in use is due in part, because there is a misperception that Ecstasy is not a dangerous drug. Only a third of twelfth graders see a "great risk" in using Ecstasy.

Is it available? You bet. In 1989, 22 percent of twelfth graders said yes, it is. In 1999, 51 percent said yes. Is it near you? Probably. Originally, it was a phenomenon of the Northeast, but now it's spreading to the North Central, South and especially the Western parts of the United States where 14 percent of the high school seniors report using the drug in the prior twelve months. National surveys of high schools reported in 2001 that over 70 percent of the schools had seniors using Ecstasy.

What Is Ecstasy, By the Way?

It is part stimulant ("speed") and part hallucinogen, similar to drugs found in oils of the natural products, sassafras and nutmeg. It is usually taken orally, but is sometimes injected or inhaled. In 1978 two chemists reported that Ecstasy produced "an easily controlled altered state of consciousness with emotional and sensual overtones," and suggested that Ecstasy might be useful in psychotherapy.

In 1985, the Drug Enforcement Administration came down decisively against the use of Ecstasy, by placing it on Schedule I of the list of Controlled Substances, citing reports of increasing recreational Ecstasy use and concern that Ecstasy might pose a threat to public health. Were they right? Here is a thumbnail sketch of the evidence since then.

What Ecstasy Does in the First Twenty-Four Hours After Use

In a dose ranging from 75 to 1200 mg over several hours, Ecstasy has the effect of releasing stored serotonin and dopamine in the brain and like speed, it accelerates the workings of the brain, heart and lungs. Like LSD, it causes a euphoria which may last four or so hours. When scientists study rats given Ecstasy using discrimination studies, the rats behave as though Ecstasy is a cross between speed and acid. A good test of whether a drug is potentially abusable is whether animals will self-administer it. Baboons and Rhesus monkeys like the stuff and some prefer it to cocaine.

The effects of Ecstasy on the body are like those of stimulants. The Ecstasy user experiences a fast heart beat, rapid respiration, elevated blood pressure, sweating and, occasionally, jaw clenching and teeth grinding. His appetite is reduced. He is more alert, which, when excessive, merges with paranoia. But the common emotion Ecstasy causes is euphoria, hence its street name. Less common reactions to the drug include nausea, vomiting, palpitations, headaches, increased reflexes, difficulty walking, urinary urgency, muscle aches, hot and cold flashes, blurred vision, insomnia and dry mouth.

A big part of the drug's popularity is due to the boost in energy it gives. Euphoria + energy + music = dancing and chemically exaggerated euphoria + energy = rave. As the body seeks to recover from these emotional and physical excesses in the next twenty-four hours, low energy, poor concentration, brooding and a letdown not so different from depression occur.

Saturday Night Fever: The Rave from a Doctor's Point of View

Huge crowds of people stimulated by loud music, lights and a drug that shifts the autonomic nervous system into racing gear, crammed into a warehouse dancing for hours, sweating profusely, dehydrating, over-hydrating, hyperventilating and exhausting themselves are the elements of a rave disaster.

Roberto, at nineteen, experienced this deadly outcome. He was already well-versed in the rave scene. He knew that the more Ecstasy he took, the higher he'd be for the longest period of time.

"Hey, Rob, you're popping E like there's no tomorrow!" laughed John one night at a local club. Indeed, Rob took Ecstasy until the early morning hours. On the way home, Roberto walked into a car door. He began to have trouble breathing. John had the sense to take him to the local emergency room, though by now Rob's body was becoming stiff, as if he had become a robot. His speech was a murmur and John listened closely as his friend now babbled incoherently.

In the emergency room Roberto's temperature was 105 degrees Farenheit. He was diagnosed with disseminated intravascular coagulopathy (DIC), a drug complication in which blood clots occur throughout the body and consume the body's natural coagulants. Without coagulants, a person bleeds uncontrollably. Five and a half hours after being admitted to the hospital, blood began to flow from Roberto's mouth and intravenous sites. Two hours later he was dead.

Roberto's death is not the only one reported from Ecstasy, though such events, thankfully, are rare. The definitive explanation of Roberto's case is not known. High fever and dehydration probably played a part. Also reasonable is that extreme dancing broke down muscle tissue, which in turn clogged his kidneys, which then touched off disseminated intravascular coagulopathy.

The amount of Ecstasy typically consumed by a single individual during a rave is variable, but some individuals report using up to ten doses (750-1250 mg) during the night and morning. A dose of 75 mg of Ecstasy peaks at two hours and is gone from the body in eight hours. Among Ecstasy's breakdown products are MDA, a neurotoxin. Most Ecstasy users report a warm euphoria during drug use and devote one night to the drug on the weekend, typically Saturday night, using the other day to recover. Using the drug more than twice a month appears to diminish the brain's pleasure on the drug.

Like other types of drug reactions, only a minority of users appears to suffer from actual drug disasters on the spot. But reports from poison centers and medical coroners confirm isolated cases of stroke (brain hemorrhaging or clots), abnormal heart beats and deranged bodily fluids leading to seizures, swelling of the brain, coma and death. This is what emergency room doctors call the syndrome of Saturday Night Fever.

This syndrome is the result of the simultaneous failure of multiple systems of the body, particularly when Ecstasy users become hot and dehydrated in crowded conditions. In this setting, users may drink fluids to replace sweat and overhydrate themselves. This is made worse by Ecstasy, which interferes with the brain's ability to regulate the fluid-retaining hormone vasopressin. Such intake leads to a life-threatening syndrome of reduced blood sodium, extreme fever (the highest reported being 109 deg F.), seizures, muscle breakdown, widespread clotting and bleeding at the same time and kidney failure. This syndrome is probably the human equivalent of "aggregation toxicity" scientists discovered in 1946 in mice when they were given amphetamine under crowded conditions. The rodents died at far higher rates than when given the drug without being crowded.

In 2004 Dr. Manish Patel and colleagues at the Emory University surveyed 102 deaths from MDMA reported to medical examiners in the United States from 1999 to 2001. In that interval they found a 400 percent increase in MDMA deaths. The victims tended to be young, white and otherwise healthy. Seventy percent of the deaths were directly drug-related, not, for example, related to auto accidents. Especially important is that a full third of the drug-related deaths had an average delay of access to medical services of 6.7 hours. In a drug reaction, a lot of bad things can happen in 6.7 hours.

This brings us to the treatment of rave victims. On Ecstasy, a person can become delirious and act in dangerous ways. Attention should be paid to control fever, blood pressure, abnormalities of fluids and body salts. The effects of shock and stroke are first-rank medical emergencies. Treating Ecstasy delirium is a job for the professionals. If your child or her friend show evidence of taking this drug, get the person to a hospital with a competent emergency staff. Fast. Fortunately, meltdowns like the one that killed Roberto are rare. However, lesser disasters can occur from Ecstasy and in greater numbers.

After the Rave

Especially troubling is that days and weeks after use, Ecstasy has been associated with adverse neuropsychiatric effects, including post-drug depression, panic attacks, paranoid psychosis, delirium, aggressive outbursts and cognitive disturbances. Sexual desire may be increased, but performance can be impaired. Rarely is Ecstasy reported to cause dependence in humans. But one survey of 329 Ecstasy users by Topp and others in 1999 found that one person in seven needed treatment for an Ecstasy-related psychological problem. This raises the question of whether the drug causes long-term changes in the brain, a subject that has been vigorously explored in animals and humans. Here is what we know.

What Animals Tell Us about Ecstasy

Ecstasy is a proven neurotoxin in rats, guinea pigs, mice, monkeys and baboons. It does nasty things to brain cells. Ecstasy given to mother rats in the human equivalent of the third trimester produces newborns who have reduced learning and memory. But the systems of the brain which have been shown to be most sensitive to the effects of Ecstasy are serotonin-based.

Serotonin is the oldest neurotransmitter in biology. It is found throughout the animal kingdom, from sea snails to humans. Serotonin is the chemical that helps the brain regulate mood, sleep, perception, appetite, sex and pain. Thus, it is a major player in those functions of the brain that govern pain and pleasure. It operates in the target systems that treat depression, anxiety and psychoses. Ecstasy specifically attacks serotonin-bearing nerve cells.

Injury to serotonin neurons in monkeys appears to be long-lived and possibly permanent. Ecstasy administration in animals leads to a persistent loss of a variety of markers specific to brain serotonin neurons. In addition, nerve cells appear to suffer damage or death of nerve cell fibers whose job is to connect with other nerve cells. These changes have been noted to persist up to seven years following last drug use.

The good news for the animal kingdom is that most rodents appear to recover from nerve fiber injury over a period of months. The bad news is that this does not appear to be the case for the primates studied so far, namely monkeys. Of course, humans are primates, too. So what does Ecstasy do in the human brain? A tougher question, but answers are coming in.

Ecstasy and the Human Brain

Like other drug studies in humans, studies of Ecstasy users tell us some things, but they have to be viewed with caution. Differences between two groups may not always be explained by the use of a study drug, since people are complex, do not have genetic homogeneity and so bring a bagful of personal traits and experiences to the laboratory that can affect the outcome. These differences between the drug and control groups can trick a researcher into thinking the study's finding was "a drug effect" when the real cause was from a difference in, for example, age, gender or nutrition.

Nonetheless, there is evidence that Ecstasy gives the user a brain-whack:

- Decreased serotonin breakdown chemicals in the spinal fluid
- Deduced serotonin-binding in PET scans of the brain, with the effect greater when a person uses more Ecstasy
- The same effect in SPECT scans of the brain
- Reduced brain blood flow three weeks after drug use (but not several months later)
- Abnormal hormone responses to a serotonin-releasing drug
- Reduced scores in visual and verbal memory, attention, verbal reasoning, along with increased impulsivity

A usual problem with such studies is the chicken or egg question: which came first, the drug or the alleged drug finding. In the Ecstasy story, that translates into whether Ecstasy caused the poor function or whether the Ecstasy users had poorer function *before* they used Ecstasy. One recent study concluded that Ecstasy lowers mental function *or* that people who use a great deal of Ecstasy have lower mental function *before* they embark on their hallucinogenic careers, a conclusion which makes a great deal of sense.

If brain damage occurs, what dose of Ecstasy is dangerous? Unfortunately for human beings, dosages of Ecstasy that lead to nerve cell injury in animals fall squarely in the range that humans use recreationally. Even a one-time use of a low dose of Ecstasy reduces brain serotonin and its main metabolite, 5-HIAA, but and this is a big but, this fact alone does not mean that injury has occurred. Changes in chemistry don't necessarily mean changes in brain structure. Certain antidepressants such as Prozac lower certain serotonin functions, while making people better. And so the jury is still out on this one.

Does Ecstasy Have a Place in Psychotherapy?

Some professionals think so, though they are a minority of the medical community. There has been only one study attempting to show that Ecstasy was helpful in psychotherapy. George Greer and Requa Tolbert reported in the Journal of Psychoactive Drugs in 1986 about their experience giving low doses of the drug to single volunteers and couples. These researchers found increased close-ness between partners in a relationship, increased emotional sensi-tivity, better insight into problems and actual issue resolution of problems.

A "good" psychotherapeutic outcome may be difficult to define, though. Drugs can vary in chemical purity. Unrecognized contaminants can alter the results. A subject or researcher who looks forward to a positive drug experiment is likely to bias the out-come with a positive report. It is a bit of a no-brainer to conclude that a drug that is known to make you feel good makes you feel good. Harkening back to my original warning at the beginning of this book, drugs are poisons. In this study, every subject experienced some undesirable physical experience. On the other hand, nine volunteers with a variety of psychiatric diagnoses related to anxiety, depression or personality troubles reported "improvement" nine months after the experiment on the average. But sixteen reported undesirable emotional symptoms: anxiety, depression, loneliness, paranoia, emotional flatten-ing, a "racing mind" or confusion, among others. Of the twenty-nine volunteers, twenty-two had jaw clenching, twenty-three had fatigue, eleven had insomnia and twenty-eight lost appetite during the session. The authors thoughtfully concluded that "presenting evidence estab-lishing the limits of its usefulness should discourage any movement to promote it as a social or psychological panacea."

Take-Home Lesson #10

1) Ecstasy use among young people is growing and is now in over 70 percent of high schools. It is cheap and available.
2) It is addictive and affects the body like a stimulant, increasing heartbeat, elevating blood pressure, rapid pulse respiration, etc.
3) There is no solid evidence Ecstasy helps emotional problems.
4) Animal and human studies show long-term changes in brain chemistry after use of Ecstasy.
5) Drug bursts in energy and mood in raves can create paranoia and have major medical complications resulting in toxicity and death.

Chapter 11

Hypnosedatives:
Sleeping for Keeps

Freddie, a drug counselor I knew, was warm, empathic and especially talented working with inner-city kids in the hospital. One night, though, he shared with me the story of Freddie the street fightin' man. That was who he was fifteen years before, when, like a real-life Matt Damon in the film, *Good Will Hunting*, he prowled the streets looking for a fight. There were two big differences. The first was that, unlike the film character, he was not a mathematical genius. The second was that he was high on barbiturates most of the time.

The pills caused him to stand on a street corner for the better part of a decade trying to score the drug or going through detox programs to clean up from it. After losing ten years of his life, Freddie finally cleaned up for good. He finished school and, like some former addicts who want to help others falling prey to drugs, became a drug counselor. We were lucky to have him.

Today, the medication Freddie abused has been largely replaced by other prescription drugs that do the same job more safely. They relieve anxiety, induce sleep and block panic. The older class of drugs used for these purposes were the barbiturates or barbs as they are likely to be called on the street. The newer class is the benzodiazepines or benzos.

The good news here is that benzodiazepines like Valium, Ativan, Klonopin and Xanax are far less lethal than the barbituates in an overdose. The bad news is that they are abusable, addictive and potentially fatal in withdrawal. If your doctor has treated you or a family member for anxiety problems, there is a good chance there is at least one bottle or more of a benzo type drug in your medicine cabinet. Ironically, parents are often in the dark about the drug dangers in their own homes, focused as we are on "street" drugs. However, in making a home safe from drug abuse by your children, your bathroom medicine cabinet is the first place to look for possible trouble.

As I indicated, the benzo class has legitimate benefits in helping people relax, relieve anxiety, block panic attacks and induce sleep. As it does with many addicting drugs, the body develops tolerance to benzos for some effects, like its sleep-inducing effect, but, happily, not the drugs' anxiety relieving effects. The problems begin at higher doses.

When I meet a person abusing hypnosedatives like the benzos, their handshake is often limp. They are cordial, slow and seem to be feeling no pain. At even higher doses, kids are sluggish and uncoordinated. Walking into the furniture is a giveaway, as are slurred speech, poor judgment and loss of inhibitions. These are the signs you should look for if you are worried that the benzodiazepine in your medicine cabinet is being used up faster than you are using it.

Taking such sedatives is equal to "eating your booze." They act like alcohol, because they operate at the same brain receptors that alcohol does. But how bad are they, really?

Laboratory tests and surveys show that benzos are not a major public health problem. If rats are offered these drugs, they take them no more often than water and far less than cocaine or heroin. Committing suicide is not as big a problem with these drugs, at least when used alone. By the year 2000 it was perceived more difficult for high school seniors to come by tranquilizers than alcohol, marijuana, LSD, Ecstasy, crack cocaine and amphetamines. That's because physicians appear to be prescribing them appropriately and the vast majority of patients take them responsibly.

But don't drop your guard just yet. For instance, Dr. Frank Slater was always a worrier. He couldn't sleep for a week when he was in elementary school and a science teacher told him that one day the sun would explode. A pediatrician recognized that Barton was a nervous wreck and prescribed a low dose of a benzodiazepine for anxiety beginning in his teen years. The treatment did everything that was needed. Frank took the drug throughout high school, college, medical school and residency in radiology. Allegedly, he never abused the drug and kept the dose in the prescribed range.

When he was hospitalized for an emergency appendectomy, no surgeon asked if he was taking any medications and Jim didn't tell, and so during the hospital stay, none was prescribed. When I first met Dr. Slater, he was throwing intravenous bottles at the hospital staff and shrieking incoherently. He was in a full-blown benzo withdrawal delirium. The tip-off to recognizing a withdrawal delirium from hypnosedatives is that the person looks a lot like Miguel going through alcohol withdrawal delirium, as described in chapter 8, without the smell of alcohol.

Dr. Slater was lucky. His withdrawal occurred inside a hospital where it could be recognized and treated. Less lucky is the addict trying to kick these drugs on her own. The bottom line for benzos is that besides being abusable, they can cause physical and behavioral dependence, including tolerance and, most importantly, potentially fatal drug withdrawals, which, along with alcohol, is the most deadly among all drug withdrawals.

Two other dangers should raise parents' concerns about sedatives they keep in their medicine cabinets. They *can* be fatal in overdoses, especially when more than one drug type is used at the same time. **If there is the slightest suspicion your kid has overdosed on sedative drugs, especially if alcohol or other drugs may also be problems, take him to the nearest emergency room.** The assessment and treatment of this life-threatening event require competent medical professionals.

The second danger is only apparent to folks who have become addicted to one drug or another, relapsed and are trying to find their way back into recovery. For these kids, sedative drugs like the benzos in a medicine cabinet, even if they are not the kids' drugs of choice, can weaken their resolve to remain sober.

There are kids holding onto sobriety by their fingernails. Nineteen million times a day they either crave drugs or get calls from dealers or other addicts inviting them "to party." Saying no is part of recovery. Saying yes is the beginning of relapse. A drug like a benzo is what I call a what-the-hell drug. The benzo is relaxing, calming. It reduces your vigilance to stay clean. When someone offers you heroin or coke or alcohol, the benzo inside you acts like a Jiminy Cricket in reverse. It says, "What the hell? Go for it!" And bingo, disaster follows.

What can a parent do to reduce the chance of this happening? Get rid of any benzos you have at home. On the other hand, you'll notice that I didn't use the word "prevent" in reference to keeping your child off such substances. Parents can try to tilt the scales in a safer direction, but they can't guarantee kids will stop being drug abusers. Kids have responsibility for getting off drugs, too.

Take-Home Lesson #11

1) Benzodiazepines like Valium, Ativan, Klonopin and Xanax are a newer class of drug prescribed for relieving anxiety, inducing sleep and blocking panic.
2) Kids who abuse them seem cordial, slow and, at higher doses, sluggish and uncoordinated.
3) They can cause physical and behavioral dependence.
4) Parents should empty their medicine cabinets of old and unnecessary medications, especially abusable agents (sedatives, narcotics and stimulants).
5) On the slightest suspicion that your child has overdosed on sedatives, go to the nearest emergency room.
6) Never ask a kid to stop sedatives "cold-turkey" without medical supervision; drug withdrawal can be fatal. Get medical help!

Chapter 12

Anabolic Steroids:
Muscles and Mood Disorders

This story was told to me by a state public health official. He recounted how a hard-driving high school coach had subscribed to the credo of Vanderbilt coach Red Sanders: "Winning isn't everything, it's the only thing." So he worked the varsity football team until they puked or dropped from exhaustion. His face was plastered in a permanent scowl, as if he never shifted gears from the mentality of years in the Marine Corps to working with teenaged boys. A winning season was the only thing in his mind the afternoon he injected each kid with an anabolic steroid. Other coaches pumped up their teams, he figured. He was only leveling the playing field. Short on needles, he used the same one for the entire team. The result was the winning season he yearned for and a cluster of cases of hepatitis C on the team as well.

This sad story illustrates the risk of hepatitis C from sharing needles. Untreated, hepatitis C can be fatal. But the steroid here was merely a vehicle for distributing the virus.

What Are Anabolic Steroids?

Anabolics are natural or synthetic male hormones which build muscle and masculinize the user. There are legitimate medical uses for anabolics, as in the treatment of anemia, muscular dystrophy and the wasting in AIDS. But kids take them to produce physical and athletic effects on the body's muscle mass that enhance their physical appearance and competitive prowess, two social values that are heavily marketed in our culture. In essence they are the burglarious tools in the sports of bodybuilding, power lifting, football and field events. They enable the user to steal victory from the drug-free competition.

Synthetic anabolics abound. They are preferred by the muscle-building crowd, since the drugs avoid the fate of rapid destruction of injected testosterone in the body. The synthetics (chemical variants of testosterone such as Android, Anavar and Durabolin, among others) can be taken at doses equivalent to 100 times the normal male hormone concentration. Some are taken by mouth. Others require injection. As with any drug, there are risks. Some are irreversible.

On July 15, 2003, Taylor Hooton, an appealing high school baseball player from Plano, Texas, committed suicide. A physician and Taylor's parents related his death to depression caused by the discontinuation of anabolic steroids. Observed Dr. Larry W. Gibbons, medical director of the Cooper Aerobics Center in Dallas, "This is a kid who was well-liked, had a lot of friends, no serious emotional problems. He had a bright future." The association between steroid use and suicide is worrisome, but not proven.

Are Your Kids at Risk for Anabolic Steroids?

Harvard researcher Dr. Harrison Pope in 2000 reported a decade old survey of Americans in which 900,000 men reported using anabolics some time in their lives. So did 150,000 women. The trend has only grown since then. Among American twelfth grade boys surveyed by Lloyd Johnston and colleagues at the University of Michigan in 2002, 4 percent reported use at some point in time. This is nearly double the use of the previous decade. Dr. Pope reported that two-thirds of kids using steroids said they started these drugs on or before the age of sixteen. Sixty-four thousand kids between the ages of twelve and seventeen reported using anabolics within the previous year. That's a quarter of all American users. Life steroid use (have you ever...?) for eighth graders was 2.5 percent in 2002 and 3.5 percent for tenth graders. An important criticism for such surveys is that kids don't always know the difference between anabolic steroids and anti-inflammatory steroids commonly used for asthma and allergies. Anti-inflammatory steroids have many effects, but they don't build muscle. We don't know if this confusion in kids being surveyed has accidentally inflated the usage figures.

Psychologist Lori Irving and her group at Washington State University surveyed 4,746 teens in 2002. This is a big study. Remember, bigger often means better in study designs (though not always). Dr. Irving's team confirmed a number of key facts about kids and steroids. First, they are *more* likely to be used by middle school kids than high schoolers. Steroid use was more common in boys (5.4 percent of the boys compared to 2.9 percent of the girls). And steroid use more often was associated with poor self-esteem, depression, suicide attempts, other drug use, eating disorders and greater participation in sports that emphasize weight and shape.

One key to anabolic use, as with any drug, is availability. Unfortunately, availability is high. From 1997 to 2001 prescriptions for anabolic steroids in the United States rose from 806,000 to 1.5 million. Anabolics can be purchased legally through the internet from many countries and then mailed to U.S. This is likely to make the U.S. Postal Service the largest importer of anabolic steroids in the country.

For decades the medical profession missed the boat on anabolic steroids. Studies mistakenly reported that their use did *not* build muscle. Wrong, because the doses of the studies were too low and given for too short a time to show that effect. Then, when complications from these drugs were reported, the medical profession had lost credibility and their use in kids and adults has risen in the last decade.

Six-pack Abs and Granite Pecs

No longer are anabolics used solely to enhance athletic performance. As Timothy Egan wrote in *The New York Times*, "They want to be buff. They want to be ripped. They want to glisten with six-pack abs and granite pecs like the hulks on Wrestlemania."

Besides steroids, a number of other types of drugs are abused. These are usually intended to gain muscle, lose fat and lose water. They are performance-enhancers and include thyroid hormones, growth hormone, DHEA androstenedione, amphetamines, Sudafed, vitamins, amino acids, protein supplements, laxatives, diuretics and insulin. This last is especially dangerous, as any insulin dependent diabetic will tell you, since an overdose leads to a rapid and often fatal fall in one's blood sugar. One patient only survived this ordeal when a quick thinking roommate carried him to an emergency room and told the ER doc one word, "Insulin." The doctor knew what to do from that point. Without that information the patient surely would have died, since the search for a cause of seizures and coma may take more time than a dying brain will give you. (The case also points out the value of your kid having smart roommates.)

Particularly dangerous among the so-called performance enhancers are alkaloids of the ephedra plant, which sometimes is called by its Chinese herbal name, *ma huang*. Technically these alkaloids (ephedrine, pseudoephedrine, phenylpropanolamine and others) are not steroids, but ephedra in recent years has earned a dubious distinction among some athletes as a product for weight loss and energy enhancement. A study by Stephen Bent and others in the 2003 Annals of Internal Medicine compared the safety of this herbal preparation with that of two others, kava and Ginkgo biloba, by counting cases of herbal poisoning at United States poison control centers. The results were striking. Ephedra accounted for 64 percent of all adverse reactions to herbs in America, but only 0.82 percent of the sales. Ephedra is highly dangerous stuff, associated with heart disease and strokes. In 2004 the Food and Drug Administration banned the sale of ephedra. The manufacturer's argument that plants are safer than drugs did not win in court. That doesn't mean your kid can't get it. It just means it's illegal to sell it.

Like ephedra, steroids have desirable physical effects. But along with a possible 12 percent increase in muscle fiber size from anabolics comes a less desirable array of possible mental effects. Users claim they experience positive emotions helpful to competitors, such as feelings of power, aggressiveness and euphoria. But users also suffer irritability to the point of irrational aggression, so-called "roid rage." Consider the case of Paul, a bond trader for whom bigger was better.

Paul's Story

Paul was by his own definition a scrawny kid in high school. He lacked the coordination of the athletes and kept out of harm's way in a tough school by using a fast mouth and faster feet. Girls were distant goddesses who looked through him as if he were glass. Before it was in to be one, Paul was a nerd. As he cruised the Internet one night he came to a site devoted to anabolic steroids. His first bottle of Depo-testosterone arrived in the mail when he was sixteen.

Hours and weeks and bottles of Depo-testosterone produced a different Paul. He was "ripped," which describes what his pectorals did to an old shirt when he flexed them. Not only his chest muscles, but every muscle in his body seemed a pumped cartoon of its former shape. His body appeared to be shaped like a wedge, narrow at the feet, broad at the thighs, still broader in the chest and neck. His thighs now rubbed together when he walked, changing his gait. He liked how he looked. He felt confident, aggressive, smart, attractive. He felt "ripped." The steroid use went on into college, grad school and his first few years as a bond trader.

Work as a trader was often a pressure cooker and Paul first attributed his "emotional meltdowns" of screaming, crying and punching his girlfriends as part of the craziness of his job. When I first saw Paul, he described how people in bars were talking about him behind his back. He feared they would beat him up if he let them. He took to carrying a gun. I warned him about drug-related paranoia. I asked him to stop the steroids and get rid of the gun. He agreed to both requests. Weeks later a former girlfriend brought him in for increasing depression. He denied feeling suicidal. The next day Paul killed himself with a gunshot wound to the head.

What Steroids Give a Kid for Free

Paul's story of steroid dependence illustrates what has been documented in good studies a number of times: the use of anabolics is associated with paranoia and mood disorders. Fortunately, with timely treatment, a paranoid steroid user can completely recover, as was described in a 2003 case by Isabel Teuber and her colleagues in Germany. In a controlled Harvard study of 160 athletes in 1994,

Pope and Katz found a good correlation between increasing weekly doses of steroids and higher percentages of manic or depressive experiences. At low doses of testosterone or its equivalent (less than 300 mg per week), psychiatric difficulties were almost absent, but at high doses (more than 1,000 mg per week) nearly half had mood disorders. Manic symptoms can include a protracted elevation in mood, grandiosity and aggression to the point of rage attacks. One in four high dose users, like Paul, will suffer depression. Psychotic users like Dr. Teuber's case can have delusions and hallucinations. Other distressing effects in a male can be sterility, testicular atrophy, acne, male pattern baldness and breast development. Fourteen to 69 percent of users become dependent.

Dr. Ann-Charlotte Eklof and her colleagues at the Huddinge University Hospital in Stockholm presented an analysis of over 25,000 anonymous calls to an anti-doping hotline about drugs in sports. The majority of calls were from gyms and concerned anabolic steroids. A treasure trove of drug reactions was uncovered. In decreasing frequency were complaints of aggressiveness, depression, acne, breast development, anxiety, impotence, atrophying testes, insomnia, fluid retention and mood disorders. Seventeen percent of the callers had adverse drug reactions, but only half of all callers were using steroids. The rest presumably were non-users who were worried by what they were seeing at the gym. That means in this large Swedish survey that a user's chance of getting into medical trouble from anabolics is one in three.

Girls Are Not Immune

Women athletes can abuse steroids, too. In a girl using anabolics, there is excess hair, clitoral hypertrophy and a deepening of her voice. If she becomes pregnant with a female fetus, the fetus will be masculinized. East German swimmer Christiane Knacke-Sommer was required by her coach to use oral steroids from the age of fifteen as she trained for the Olympics. Doping with anabolics paid off. She won a Bronze Medal, but at a terrible price. In her words, the drug destroyed her body and her mind. In a scandal that only begins to reveal the extent of drugs in sport, other women athletes in East Germany came forward with reports of masculinization, deformed babies, tumors, liver disorders and depression.

What Controlled Studies Tell Us about Anabolic Steroids and Health

Beyond case reports such as Paul's and Christiane's there are a few controlled studies comparing users and non-users on a variety of outcome measures. Miia Parssinen and Timo Seppala from the National Public Health Institute in Helsinki, Finland, in 2002 described the three most important health risks from steroids: heart disease mental illness and a possible increased risk for cancer. Dr. Parssinen's group compared 62 male Finnish weightlifting champions and 1,094 controls for twelve years. In that time frame the lifters were nearly five times more likely to die: three had heart attacks; three committed suicide; and two had died from liver disease and cancer respectively.

Steroids and the Olympics

If a high jumper in the Olympics installed springs on his feet and then claimed a gold medal, he would be laughed out of the community of world class athletes. But an equivalent form of cheating occurs in a small number of would-be winners by the use of performance enhancing drugs. In 1967 the International Olympic Medal Commission began to ban such drugs for the first time following a steady stream of evidence documenting drug abuse, overdoses and positive drug screens. At the University of Illinois Medical Center, Dr. Heather Prendergast and colleagues analyzed drug tests of Olympians from 1972 to 2002 and reported their findings in 2003. Seventy cases of doping among Olympians were found. The most common agent abused was steroids, followed by stimulants, diuretics, beta-2 agonists and beta blockers. The countries with the greatest number of doping cases were Bulgaria and the United States, each with seven. The most common sports associated with doping were:

1. weightlifting
2. track and field
3. skiing
4. wrestling
5. volleyball
6. pentathlon

    7. cycling
    8. swimming
    9. gymnastics
    10. rowing

I spell these out explicitly to give parents a heads-up in terms of risk. And remember, the list is not comprehensive. American-style football is not an Olympic sport, but American teens looking for an edge on the playing field are at risk. The use of steroids in professional baseball is an enduring controversy. To a modest extent in the Olympics there has emerged a cat and mouse game between doping athletes and the twenty-nine IOC accredited laboratories around the world assigned the task of detecting drugs. Scientists including Pascal Kintz at the Institut de Medicine Legale in Strasbourg, France are increasingly confident that sophisticated techniques like analyzing hair for drug use can uncover drug use occurring years before. But the work of Cristiana Gambelunghe and co-workers at the University of Perugia in Italy in 2002 found that certain naturally occurring steroids could be increased simply by physical effort. Clearly all the answers about sports and steroids are not in, but there's no point in a parent turning a blind eye to a kid who is bulking up out of a bottle.

Warning Signs: What Parents Should Do and Look Out For
Take-Home Lesson #12

1) Anabolic steroids are natural or synthetic male hormones used to build muscle.
2) Heed the warning signs of a kid drifting into anabolic use: muscle enhancing vitamins and minerals, excessive time in weight training, receiving international packages and utilizing needles or syringes.
3) Confront the kid who seems driven to pump up.
4) Address the issue in any kid involved in a high-risk sport like football, wrestling or weight lifting.
5) Any kid using needles is at high risk for hepatitis C and at some risk for HIV infection and must be checked for these conditions by a physician.
6) Users of steroids may develop protracted mood elevation, rage attacks, pyschosis and depression.

Chapter 13

Psychostimulants: Coke and Speed

Margot was the life of the party, a cheerleader, voted most popular in her high school class. She was a risk taker. The weekend rush of cocaine had all of the thrills and none of the spills of the rest of her senior year in high school. She continued to snort coke through college, at first limiting the substance to Friday and Saturday nights and using Sundays to recover for the school week. However, Fridays spread to Thursdays and Thursdays to Wednesdays, until she was asked to leave school.

She moved in with Tommy, her boyfriend, a pre-law student with little interest in drugs. Margot's interest in coke, however, only increased. Tommy was angry and confused coming home to an apartment of crack pipes and uninvited guests. When Margot forged his name on checks and smoked up the money, he was enraged. When she forged his name to the title of his truck and sold it for cocaine, he threw her out.

"I put his truck up my nose," Margot told me ruefully in the emergency room that night. She refused to go into detox and only wanted "some drugs" for her nerves. It was the last time I would see her for months, as she chose the life of a "couch commando," moving from one apartment to another trading sex for cocaine.

How Cocaine Became a Drug of Horror

People began using cocaine at least 2500 years ago to get high and outrun their enemies and prey. It was relatively safe, because our aboriginal ancestors chewed the stuff slowly. They didn't inject or snort it as chemically refined powder. The botanical form of cocaine offered a dose that was hundreds if not thousands of times weaker than the street drug. This led to the mistaken belief that refined coke was safe.

However, refined coke was the addiction that unhinged Sigmund Freud and the surgical pioneer, William Halsted. If two of the smartest physicians in history fell into the trap of cocaine use, what chance does the average kid have against this drug? In terms of kids at risk, we can ask the question another way. Of the eight percent of high school seniors who use coke, how many will get addicted? We have a good idea: roughly one in six.

Kids and Coke

Coke began making its presence known in hospital emergency rooms in the 1970s. By the mid 1980s, the drug cartels had increased production, resulting in falling drug prices and rising use. This epidemic of drug use brought with it overdoses, drug crimes and "crack babies," increased political pressure for governmental intervention and in America was the impetus for the "War on Drugs." Use of cocaine is a crime and addicts are felons.

Despite the War, the general trend of cocaine use among high school kids, householders and arrestees (three frequently surveyed populations), has been stable in the past ten years. Eight percent of high school seniors and 4 percent of eighth graders have used coke at least once. Near the peak of the cocaine epidemic, the National Comorbidity Survey found 2.7 percent cocaine dependence among the 16 percent of the fifteen-to-fifty-four-year olds who reported cocaine use. That's roughly a 17 percent risk of developing addiction among users or one in six.

Crack and Coke

These terms mean the same from the brain's point of view, since they are both forms of the drug cocaine. But the snowy white powder, cocaine hydrochloride, is easily dissolved in water and so can be abused by injection or dissolving in one's nasal secretions. Try to smoke it, however and most of the drug is destroyed by the heat. Users then discovered that the freebase form of cocaine can be smoked since it sublimates in the air before it burns and so becomes available to the lungs and brain. The freebase originally was made by cooking the drug with alkali and extracting it with organic solvents. Such solvents are highly flammable and accidental fires, such as the one that afflicted comic genius, Richard Pryor, led to a safer method of preparing the freebase. This is done by cooking cocaine with sodium bicarbonate until it becomes a white, smokable mass, crack. Crack or freebase cocaine and impurities gets its name from the crackling sound the substance emits when it is smoked.

The distinction between cocaine powder and crack is more than academic. Sparked in part by the cocaine death of basketball player Len Bias in 1986, Federal lawmakers passed five year minimum sentences for cocaine possession and trafficking. The criteria are possession of at least 500 grams of powder cocaine, or at least *five grams* of crack. Five grams is the weight of a nickel. Thus, an inner city African American with a small amount of crack in his pocket is sentenced as stiffly as a white dealer with $40,000 worth of powder in his briefcase. The result has been a disparity in criminal justice in which African Americans receive disproportionate jail time. The United States Sentencing Commission was created by Congress in 1984 to develop guidelines to reduce such disparities. In 1997 it recommended reducing the 100:1 sentencing ratio to a ratio of 5:1 by weight. In a misguided spirit of "getting tough on drugs," Congress rejected the USSC's recommendation, preferring to continue the Federal policy of punishing the patient. Efforts go on to correct this form of racial discrimination.

The Kid on Coke

He has increased energy beyond the normal high of teenagers. He's more alert, less hungry and unable to sleep. He's high, vigilant, even suspicious and paranoid. He's hyperactive, talkative and grandiose. On large doses of cocaine, he may see and hear things that you don't. These are hallucinations. It is time to bring in reinforcements in the form of a medical consultation then and there. A visit to the local emergency room is indicated to properly figure out what's going on and start the young person on the correct path of treatment. Do not wait for your son or daughter to get to this stage before acting. Instead confront the kid having weird moods directly; ask for drug testing from the kid's physician (cocaine products can be found in the urine as long as four days after use). Get an emergency assessment of a kid who is not acting like himself.

What the Dealer Doesn't Tell Your Kid

Reports of professional basketball players, television comics and movie stars dying from cocaine overdoses and medical complications are not the major problem. Not everyone who uses cocaine drops dead from cardiac arrhythmia. The odds are low. But they are not zero. Neither is the risk zero for cocaine-related tics, uncontrollable writhing, coronary artery spasms, heart attacks and inflammation, lung collapses, headaches, strokes, ruptured aortas, muscle breakdown, renal failure and infections including HIV, hepatitis B and hepatitis C. One in four heavy users has seizures.

They Gotta Have It

Nevertheless, addicts say they need the drug and so they feel, from centers deep in the brain. This is the first lesson in dealing with an addicted kid or adult, for that matter. Every thought, word and deed of the untreated addict is *how to get more drugs*. This is the behavioral heart of the disease of addiction. It's also the source of much confusion and heartache for the addict's family. Noted drug expert Dr. Jerome Jaffe calls this the "purposive syndrome," where every communication from an addict has as its main purpose feeding the habit. Thus, promises to take that tuition check herself directly to the school's bursar or cash in his savings account to get a car to get to that job, etc., etc., more often lead to disaster than not. A parent's response to purposive behavior is simple: Be skeptical of any behavior which can lead to drug buys.

Addiction occurs when voluntary becomes obligatory. For instance, Roger, who has been addicted to coke for the last eight months, has a set daily routine. His day begins in the afternoon, as he awakens with a crashing mood from the previous night's crack. He is thin, unshaven, dirty and coughing a bit. The depression and emptiness in his brain is being offset by another message that grows louder with each minute. He is craving cocaine. His mind is struggling with the options of the afternoon and evening. How can he come up with enough money for another night of crack?

He has already lied to his family, cheated his friends and stolen from retailers for drug money. Selling drugs to his remaining friends is possible, but his addiction has reached the point that his dealer will not trust him with a supply of the drug for resale. Roger will spend his day trying to find a wholesale lot of marijuana, which he can then sell in order to buy the precious cocaine. If he is successful in his business efforts, that night he will smoke crack again or shoot coke intravenously, risking HIV and hepatitis C. Then he will crash into a stuporous depression with suicidal ideation when the coke is gone. And so the cycle will continue until Roger becomes too sick to keep going, gets help for himself or dies. Roger's parents can only do so much. They can bring him to a detoxification center and rehabilitation program. They can't make him want to recover.

Where Does This Addiction Come From?

First, we know that genes are a factor. When one identical twin is cocaine dependent, his twin is more likely to be dependent as well, compared to when one of a pair of fraternal twins is dependent. But this is not the only source of vulnerability, since environment is a hugely important factor as well. How so? First, drug availability is huge. Why do some movie stars and sports figures take drugs which cost a fortune when they become addicted? One reason is they can afford to. As actor Robin Williams said, "Cocaine is God's way of saying you're making too much money."

However, coke is also God's way of saying you don't make enough money. Cocaine production and sales is often the industry of first choice in developing countries for want of less socially destructive ways of earning money. In American ghettos drug dealing is risky, but an escalator for the economically disadvantaged, because dealing is a rapid rise to the top for folks who don't have too many other ways to get there. A third factor for the cycle of addiction, recovery and relapse is chronic stress, which now can be measured in terms of changes in one of the brain's stress hormones, CRF. But in the United States, the most shameful cause for drug relapse is our policy of supporting punishment over treatment.

Cocaine and Mental Illnesses

The drug dealer doesn't tell your kid about psychiatric comorbidity, the mental illnesses associated with cocaine, such as depression, panic disorder, mania and schizophrenia. About half of all cocaine-dependent persons suffer major depressions at least once in their lives. Cocaine increases the risk for panic disorder fourteen times and the risk for mania twelve times. Kids with schizophrenia who use cocaine just make themselves sicker. It's not always easy to figure out which comes first, cocaine dependence or the other mental illness. But in either case, both should be treated at the same time. To only deal with the addiction is to let the mental illness freewheel out of control.

Kids with antisocial personality disorders use coke more, but not all coke users who commit crimes have personality disorders. Rather, dependence on coke can lead decent kids into crime to support their habits. Cocaine is a crime drug. Among adolescents committing serious crimes, 40 percent were committed by the 1.3 percent who used cocaine. While this is a sorry statistic, parents should not forget, even though recent events in your kids' lives have made them feel overwhelmed, that treatment for cocaine addiction works — not 100 percent, not necessarily with lifelong abstinence, but enough to save lives and infuse them with dignity.

Speed

Speed, the street name given to the amphetamine family of drugs, are kissin' cousins of cocaine. These drugs reduce fatigue, create euphoria and increase alertness. They have been used by long-distance truckers, students, homemakers and high achievers under pressure to produce in the entertainment and business worlds.

Alertness carried to an extreme results in paranoia, as occurred with Ryan, who used a prescribed amphetamine for ten days, then murdered his five-week-old daughter with a shotgun, because the voice of God told him "to send her to Heaven."

A particularly popular member of the speed family is methamphetamine, with effects similar to cocaine but lasting six to thirty times longer. Under the street names of Crank, Go, Crystal and Ice, the drug is smoked and is common in the American West. Like cocaine, it increases blood pressure and heart rate while decreasing appetite and the need for sleep. Higher doses lead to anxiety, irritability and paranoia as well as cardiac and lung toxicity. Rats, when given an unlimited supply of methamphetamine, will take it until it kills them.

Dr. Edythe London and her colleagues at the University of Southern California in Los Angeles published a study in 2004 which used PET scans in abstinent methamphetamine users. They found abnormal metabolism in the brain which correlated with the symptoms of depression and anxiety that speed users suffer even when they're drug-clean. In addition to methamphetamine, other usual suspects of the speed family are amphetamine, Dexedrine and Ritalin.

These last have come under scrutiny recently, because they are used to treat kids with ADHD (attention deficit hyperactivity disorder). In ADHD kids these drugs paradoxically quiet them down and improve mental focus. Drug critics say that we are drugging our children to control them in school. While this abuse of psychiatry is possible, the amphetamines are a two-edged sword with a legitimate place in psychiatry, including their use for kids with ADHD. With this problem children have slightly smaller brain volumes than other kids. The argument that medical treatment causes the brain changes in ADHD is false, since, in 2002, Dr. Xavier Castellanos at the Child Study Center of NYU found that ADHD kids had smaller brains than other kids *before* they were medicated for ADHD. The good news is that by age fifteen such differences between the groups completely disappeared, suggesting a good outcome if kids are caught early and helped through a difficult time in their early educational years.

However, not every hyperactive kid in a classroom has ADHD. Children need a good diagnosis before treatment and that means careful evaluation. The fear of drug addiction from prescribed stimulants for ADHD is misplaced. An overburdened, under-responsive school will do far more damage to these kids when ADHD goes untreated. It is a rare kid who abuses Ritalin, rarer still with good parental controls. In fact, a dozen studies, most recently in 2003 by Russell Barkley and colleagues in the medical journal *Pediatrics*, show that prescribed Ritalin in kids does *not* lead to drug abuse in later life. But the treatment of children with psychoactive drugs is, well, in its infancy. That means the data needed to guide us regarding safety and efficacy are just beginning to come in. One cautionary study suggests the complexity of the issue. Dr. William Carlezon and his group at Harvard in 2003 found that normal rats given stimulant drugs as pups continued to have behavioral changes as adults. Some appeared good (less responsiveness to cocaine) and some appeared not so good (more depression-like behavior). This is important, but not the whole story. Rats aren't human. They can't really tell you if they're depressed. And a kid with ADHD may not have a nervous system like kids without it. As a mentor used to yell at me when I showed him an inconclusive research finding, "More data!"

Helping the Chemically Stimulated Kid

For both cocaine and speed, problems of depression and psychosis usually clear within a week of abstinence. Treatment for dependence can be effective. Typically, at one-year post treatment, cocaine use can fall by 94 percent. Here are basic principles for the treatment of these kids.

- Start in the least restrictive environment. That means begin in an outpatient setting if you can. Then progress to inpatient and long-term rehabilitation settings if you must. Increase intensity of treatment with each relapse.
- Individualize care over the long run. No two kids are alike.
- Treat psychiatric illnesses early on.
- The most positive factor on outcome is the *length* of treatment, not the type of treatment. Stay with it!
- Stick with treatments that are tried and true.
- Pursue new treatments if there is evidence to support them. (Promising drug treatments include the use of naltrexone, propranolol, clozapine, phentermine and dextromethorphan. In 2004, the National Institute on Drug Abuse reported new evidence that disulfiram, useful in alcoholism, was also helpful with cocaine addiction.)

Remember that the success of treatment will be a victory of the kid's spirit, not her or his chemistry. The figures for recovery from stimulant dependence compare favorably to treatment for other medical conditions such as heart attacks, high blood pressure and depression.

Margot, of whom I spoke earlier, is a good example of someone who was addicted but found successful treatment. She sold body and soul for cocaine, but there were a few silver linings around her clouds. One was that she had not used intravenous drugs and so had not contracted HIV or hepatitis C. Another was a family that hung in there for her. The third was her former boyfriend who had the good sense to bring her to the hospital when she showed up at his doorstep begging for "a loan."

Margot's recovery began there or perhaps when she realized that in the lingo of recovery, she had "hit bottom." First she entered detox, then treatment for depression and then months of rehabilitation at the local Salvation Army under lock and key. She entered a twelve-step program and turned to its wisdom time and again to fight back her months of craving. The last time I saw Margot she was clean, nourished and working as an assistant manager in a dress store. She smiled warmly when we spoke. She had been clean for seven months, attended her twelve-step program each day and had just been readmitted to college. Recovery is always a walk on thin ice. Bravo to her for each step she takes.

Take-Home Lesson #13

1) Crack cocaine is among the most rapidly addictive substances known.
2) Kids on coke have increased energy, are less hungry and need less sleep.
3) Suspicion, paranoia, hyperactivity, grandiosity and hallucinations are symptoms of heavy coke use.
4) If your child has these symptoms, he or she needs a medical consultation and drug testing now.
5) Tics, coronary spasms, lung collapses, renal failure, seizures and infections including HIV, hepatitis B and C are risks of heavy cocaine use.
6) Speed, a relative of coke, reduces fatigue, increases alertness, but also may lead to anxiety, irritability and paranoia.
7) Amphetamines like Ritalin are legitimate treatments for kids with attention deficit hyperactivity disorder (ADHD) where they can improve mental focus.
8) Not every hyperactive kid has ADHD and each child needs expert diagnosis before treatment.

9) Depression and psychosis problems, which occur after speed and cocaine use, usually clear in one week of non-use.

10) First try outpatient care, then inpatient and lastly, rehabilitation for your cocaine-addicted kid.

Chapter 14

Narcotics: Pills to Needles

Waldo's Senior Year

Like some other seventeen-year-olds, Waldo is experienced with marijuana and cocaine, but new to the world of injectables. Prom night changes that. Waldo's first experience shooting heroin, like many others', occurs when a friend injects him. Like his hero John Travolta in the film, *Pulp Fiction,* Waldo slips into a euphoric high, a brief burst of energy and then sleepiness. Half-asleep and half-awake, his pupils constrict to the size of pins. His breathing slows. He spends a great deal of time looking at his shoe. When he speaks, he mumbles. He will have little memory of events going on around him while he is high. With little forethought, Waldo has crossed into the dangerous world of narcotics users.

From Pills to Needles, with Smoke In Between

Narcotics have been around for thousands of years. As scholar Gregory Austin notes, the botanical form, opium, contributed to the nineteenth century Opium Wars between Britain and China in which Britain insisted on the right of the British East India Company to sell opium in China despite the strenuous objections of the Chinese government. Originally eaten or smoked, opium has been transformed into the modern narcotics codeine, morphine, Demerol and heroin, among others. OxyContin is a narcotic and responsible for the recent spate of drugstore crimes, overdoses and Rush Limbaugh's downfall. These drugs are a long way from the lustrous poppy that spawned them. They are relatively pure, have high potency and can be eaten, smoked and injected. This is where much of the trouble begins, since street "doses" vary widely, as does drug tolerance among users and not every addict thinks twice before using a dirty needle. The result? Accidental overdoses, AIDS and hepatitis C.

How Many of Our Kids Are at Risk?

There are legal opioid drugs, containing codeine, oxycodone and hydrocodone, which are commonly prescribed for pain and illegal narcotics, like heroin. The notion that heroin is worse than legal narcotics depends on where you sit. As Senator Susan Collins from Maine observed in 2004, in many states death from prescription drug overdoses now exceed deaths from illegal one.

The imagery in the popular press of heroin chic, emaciated models and Uzi-packing ghetto dealers does not do justice to the threat of narcotics. Yes, heroin is in the inner city, but it is also in the suburbs. Over the last decade about 2 percent of high school seniors have used heroin and almost as many eighth graders have as well. That figure rises as kids leave school, so that 5 percent of young adults between eighteen and twenty-five become heroin users. Heroin is no respecter of social class. Addiction strikes at every economic level. A kid can become addicted to heroin in a week or two. The same thing can happen with the opioids from the medicine cabinet. Fortunately, most drug experimenters wise up before that point.

Narcotics and a Kid's Brain

To understand drug abuse, addiction and the pathways to recovery, parents need to know what happens to a kid who is getting high on heroin. Narcotics like heroin operate on a tiny part of the brain, which then releases the molecule, dopamine. It's the dopamine that makes a user high. But dopamine circuits are also thought to be related to *all* positive reinforcers, including food, sex and learning. Narcotics mess with some of the most basic machinery that makes us tick.

The tiny part of the brain where heroin operates is the *nucleus accumbens*. It connects widely to the sensing, thinking and feeling part of the brain. When dopamine floods the brain's synapses, the brain is happy, feeling high. When the heroin supply runs out, dopamine shuts off, the brain becomes awash in stressful overactivity and mechanisms to relieve distress roll into action. To do this, large regions of the nervous system are recruited for just one purpose: to get more drug. This is what makes an addict act the way he does. We described it with cocaine. It's the *purposive syndrome*. Even more devilish is that many addicts report that they seek the drug "to feel normal again," the way they felt *before* they got hooked. However, heroin withdrawal is another matter.

Waldo, Dependent

Waldo, who became dependent on heroin, experienced this problem. Not having a steady supply, despite his best purposive efforts to score the drug often, he found himself in a cycle of getting high and withdrawing. The street euphemism for withdrawal symptoms is "Jonesing," a euphemism for the rush of overactivity in his brain and body once heroin drains out of it.

In the emergency department of a local hospital where he hoped to be admitted for a drug detox, Waldo's bowels cramped in pain. He had watery diarrhea. He vomited once earlier and had been suffering nausea all day. He was yawning, tearing, sweating and trembling. His pupils were large. He tried to sleep, with no success. His muscles ached in his back, arms and legs. His thoughts of cleaning up were offset by persistent images of his dealer, his junk buddies, syringes, needles and his beloved heroin. He made for the front door at least three times, telling himself he was only going for a cigarette. A savvy emergency room nurse keeping an eye on him wasn't sure he'd come back. She'd seen it before. As bad as it sounds, opiate withdrawal is not fatal, just miserable. Waldo's brain was afire with the message, "Find the drug!" This is drug craving. Craving, too, will not kill you. However, Waldo the addict has a twenty-fold risk of dying prematurely compared to his drug-free peers. Before that happens, he may embark on a career that runs for decades in which every act is aimed at finding more drugs. This is how parents come to hate their addicted child.

During their time battling their son's disease, Waldo's parents' found him nodding out in a drug haze in his room more times than they can remember. They had hired lawyers to get him out of jail, counselors to put him on the right path and psychiatrists with a variety of therapies. They drove him to Alcoholics Anonymous, Narcotics Anonymous and group therapies with dedicated psychologists. They had waited for long hours in emergency rooms, neglecting their other children, to be told that their son was going to survive yet another drug overdose. Then they went home relieved he was alive and hating him for what he had done to their lives. Yes, Waldo's parents hated him and secretly wished he had died in the room where he was found. And then they hated themselves for thinking that, felt guilty and then tried to make it up to him by enabling his drug use all over again. Don't fall into this terrible trap. You can hate the disease, but you don't have to hate the child.

How You Live as an Addict

In the absence of treatment, opiate addiction becomes a career. It often lasts into middle age or longer. It can be marked by periods of being clean and periods of addiction. It also is often marked by chronic disruption in one's life path, with broken families, stunted careers, poor health and impoverishment.

How You Die as an Addict

A common way is by overdose. This may result from a new user trying a drug far stronger than his brain is accustomed to or an experienced user adding a second or third drug to a potent dose of heroin. Common fatal combos found with narcotics at autopsy include alcohol, cocaine and sedatives.

Death by infection with HIV and now hepatitis C figures prominently in the media. After overdose, AIDS is the second commonest cause of death in intravenous drug users. Yet both HIV and hepatitis C infections are preventable. The cost of indifference to this issue is incalculable. Infected addicts transmit the HIV virus sexually into the non-drug using population.

Recently about 70 percent of all intravenous drug users have become infected with hepatitis C, a progressive, potentially fatal illness which slowly destroys the liver. There is treatment, but no guarantee that it will be successful. More dismaying, hepatitis C patients who undergo liver transplants often become reinfected by the same virus they were trying to escape. The virus is passed to the fetus from an infected mother 5 percent of the time, even if she has only used intravenous drugs in the distant past. It is estimated that about five million Americans have hepatitis C. Even with the perfection of transplant technique, there simply will not be enough livers available for transplant when these patients develop symptoms in the next two decades. Another problem of hepatitis C is that it is often present in the absence of symptoms. That means there are likely to be millions of people who are silently infected with hepatitis C today and for want of a diagnosis are going untreated while the disease progresses.

My patient, Margaret, a successful attorney, came to me for treatment of depression. She told me that as a wild teen she had shared a needle once with friends experimenting with narcotics. That was it. No addiction, no booze or drug career, no school drop-outs. Two months before seeing me, her internist noticed mildly elevated liver tests on a routine exam. Liver biopsy showed fibrosis, the microscopic evidence of cirrhosis—and hepatitis C virus in her blood. In the absence of other explanations, it is more than likely Margaret's hepatitis C was acquired the one time she injected a drug as a teenager. Margaret is not my only patient living out such a story.

The dangerous illnesses of hepatitis C and AIDS can be prevented on a number of fronts. These include an aggressive public health commitment to drug treatment and drug abstinence; the reduction of needle use with methadone maintenance and the removal of septic needles from communities with needle exchange programs. At this point, these life saving ideas have been resisted or ignored by local and national governments on the mistaken belief that reducing drug harm with methadone or needles might foster addiction. No good evidence supports this prejudice. So can parents make a difference here? Absolutely! Remember, medical problems are social problems. And politically active parents can make a difference.

How Parents Can Fight for Their Kids against Narcotics

The key places to start are:

- The medicine cabinet. Get rid of old, out of date and no longer needed pain medications. Do it now.
- Your kid's friends. Keep an eye out for those kids who show obvious signs of being stoned, talking excessively of drugs, having the nickname of a reptile or a cell phone for an address. Bite the bullet. Confront your kid early and often. Try something like, "Tell me something about your friend, Snake."
- People in the home who suffer chronic pain and cancer. Doctors often prescribe narcotics for them and they should. But having narcotics float about the house in an uncontrolled manner invites kids to experiment, experimenters to become dependent and kids in recovery to relapse. Narcotics are called controlled substances for a reason. Control them.
- Health professionals at home. Despite regulations to the contrary, narcotics can appear in the homes of doctors, dentists, nurses and other health professionals for a host of legitimate reasons. For a parent, the bottom line is to control them and only let them into the house when there is a current reason, not a hypothetical one.
- Get over denial. Any physical evidence of narcotic drug use (needles, track marks, a positive drug screen in blood or urine) is a call to battle. This kid needs 1) a sit-down type confrontation, 2) a visit to a physician and 3) a psychiatric assessment, for starters.

A few more words are in order about the perils in the medicine cabinet. In recent years the misuse of narcotic-based painkillers, sold as e.g., Vicodin, OxyContin and Percocet, among teens and young adults has doubled, up to 13.2 percent of all surveyed high school seniors in 2003, according to data from Lloyd Johnston and his University of Michigan team. Drug companies are now at work to chemically alter their narcotic products to prevent them from being snorted or shot intravenously. But this is a classic argument for Heads-up Parenting. Which is more desirable? Waiting for a drug company to insert pepper oil into painkillers (one current idea to discourage snorting) or cleaning out the family medicine cabinet regularly?

Parents and Treatment

Remember, as I've pointed out before, drug treatment works! As a parent with a drug abusing kid, you need to commit yourself to it for your child as much as you can. Be aware that recovery from narcotics dependence is long, hard, slow, painful and possible. The three classic pitfalls for the addicted kid remain: people, places and things. Keep this in mind and you will be able to watch out for signs of your child's risk of relapse. People who are in the drug world, places where drugs are obtainable and things which facilitate relapse such as other drugs (alcohol, benzos and marijuana are classics) are all triggers for relapse.

The basic principles of addiction recovery described in the previous chapter and ahead in chapter 18, "When Kids Are Addicts," apply here as well. The goal of treatment is minimize drug use over time. The essential strategy for relative abstinence is to recruit the rest of the brain to fight back against the jammed signal from the tiny part that incessantly urges, "Use...use...use!" This tactic takes daily effort: through self-help groups, drug counseling, psychotherapy, medications for psychiatric illnesses and the power of the courts.

Take-Home Lesson #14

1) Heroin use occurs in the inner city and suburbs in a small number of high school kids, but the same percentage of junior high school kids.
2) Heroin and other narcotics affect a tiny part of the brain, releasing dopamine and creating a high.
3) Among the effects of withdrawal may be: nausea, large pupils, sleeplessness and muscle aches.
4) Potentially fatal combinations include cocaine, alcohol and sedatives.
5) Beware, in addition to HIV, an epidemic of hepatitis C is infecting the majority of intravenous drug users.
6) Remember, recovery from narcotics dependence is long and painful but possible.

Chapter 15

Odd Ducks, Street Turkeys
and Other Uncommon Fowl

After smoking angel dust for an afternoon, eighteen-year-old Tyrone set himself on fire. It was an accident, his friends said. They had been smoking dust, or PCP, and getting high in a garage. Tyrone was laughing like everyone else. Then he got excited. He tried to squirt the vampires he saw with burning lighter fluid. He wasn't making sense. He was yelling. It was goofy seeing him stagger about squirting lighter fluid on the floor and tossing matches. When the fluid ran out, he used a canister of gasoline. The flames leapt from the floor to the wall, then from the wall to his clothes splashed with gas. No one thought to help. Angel Dust is a veterinary anesthetic. No one remembered hearing Tyrone cry out as his friends ran from the garage. He succumbed to third degree burns several weeks later. There are many hard lessons from this death, but one is the destructive potential of some of the rarer drugs on the street. I call these drugs odd ducks, street turkeys and other uncommon fowl, because they are limited crowd pleasers for a number of reasons:
- Too dangerous (e.g., PCP)
- Too mild (e.g., cough syrups)

- Too weird (e.g., antifreeze, toad skins)
- Too rare (e.g., obscure South American hallucinogens)
- Too new (e.g., GHB)

They do not often qualify as major public health problems and usually have not caught on as the drug de jour. Yet they can be the drugs of first choice for misinformed kids or the drugs of last resort among the desperate. To the experienced addict, these are junk drugs and likely the origin of the word junkie for addict. Odd duck drugs which I think are important for parents to look out for include:

- Inhalants
- PCP
- GHB
- Designer drugs
- Exotic plants

Pop Quiz: What is a junk drug?

Answer: One that even an addict believes does more harm than good.

Typical of junk drugs of the last century are the industrial alcohols. These are toxic alcohols like methanol added to drinking alcohol to keep the employees from partying on the job, a strategy of prevention by poisoning. Methanol at a dose of 1/3 of an ounce causes blindness.

Would anyone drink such stuff? Yes, but only a desperate alcoholic craving a drink and unable to buy one or a kid who didn't know any better. Other drinks of desperation include antifreeze and rubbing alcohol, junk drugs since they are poisons in small doses. Thankfully, their use is rare. Unfortunately, that is not the case with inhalants, which for United States and European teens are the junkers in widest use.

Inhalants: The VOCs Populi

Inhaled chemicals are called volatile organic compounds or VOCs, on the labels of glues and aerosols. Kids get high when they inhale VOCs. These substances are surprisingly popular. One eighth grader in five has experimented with them. This is a huge number. Boys abuse them far more than girls. Inhalants are in the garages and closets of many homes, in the form of glues, paints, gas fuels and propellants in aerosol cans. Fatalities have been reported in kids as young as age eight. The majority of deaths occur in kids with an average age of sixteen.

Harvey had a major problem with these substances. His junior high school acquaintances called him Huffer Boy, because of his history of breathing, or "huffing," aerosols from glue and spray paints. He came to school with pale face, matted hair, vacant blue eyes and his clothes reeked of glue and spray paint. His mother later said she thought he was only spraying graffiti. His grades were poor. A brother was addicted to heroin and in and out of the house. His father, a commercial fisherman, had abandoned his family when his wife was pregnant with Harvey. Sniffing glue squeezed into plastic food storage bags first made the eighth grade bearable.

Then the sniffing became a daily event. Harvey stole the raw materials of his euphoria from hardware stores, spraying a can of paint into a bag, sealing the bag over his face and breathing deeply until he hallucinated. The last time he huffed paint, he taped the bag in place so that he could free his arms and lie back in the incinerator room of his apartment building enjoying the trip. But the rig deprived him of oxygen. The toluene intoxicated his brain so that the alarm signals of asphyxiation went unheeded. In waves of toluene, carbon dioxide and the fading images of hallucinations, he suffocated in his sleep.

This tragic story illustrates that abusing inhalants is a desperate, dirty and dangerous business. So why do kids do it? They do it because inhalants are legal to have, cheap, easy to get, easy to use, easy to hide and can bring a perverse reward as a ticket into the occasional social group. Twenty breaths of a volatile organic compound like 1 percent gasoline can lead to several hours of intoxication. As with any other drug, however, intoxication is not all you get from inhalants.

Inhalants Damage a Kid's Mind and Body

Manufacturers of VOCs for years benignly told parents to keep spray cans "Out of Reach of Children," as if the average beanpole teenager couldn't keep a can of spray paint out of his mother's reach. Such disingenuous warnings were replaced in response to the Federal Hazardous Substance Act of 1995, so that a typical can of spray adhesive carries two or three paragraphs of warnings, along with a phone number for the company if there is trouble. However, labels are certainly not preventing VOC abuse by kids. For this, Heads-up parents are required and knowing the medical effects of inhalants is important.

Acute effects of VOCs on a kid's brain include: motor stimulation at low doses and motor suppression at higher doses, loss of balance, decreases in perception, memory and manual dexterity, headaches, irritation of the linings of a kid's throat and bronchi, thirst, abdominal pain, nausea and vomiting blood, sleepiness, coma and suffocation.

One of the key tests of the addictive potential of a drug is whether an animal will self-administer it. VOCs pass this test. Kids, too, can develop dependence on VOCs after repeated use, with dire physical consequences. In the VOC-addicted kid there may be widespread brain atrophy, hearing loss, the effects of lead poisoning, seizures, lower IQs and irreversible damage to his liver, kidneys and muscles.

The Stink Test

How can a parent tell if a kid is fooling around with VOCs? Do the Stink Test. If he stinks, his room stinks or his clothes stink (Moms have better noses than Dads), a flag has been raised. If you can smell the VOC, more often than not it's abusable, especially if it comes from propellants in spray cans, gaseous fuels, solvents for glues, thinners for paints and typing correction fluids. Chemically, these VOCs are hexane, methane, toluene, methylbutyl ketone, trichloroethylene, trichloroethane, dichloromethane, butane, leaded and unleaded gasolines.

If you find inhalant paraphernalia (rags, plastic bags, sources of chemicals) in your child's room, or tucked in odd places in the home, the big three steps of Heads-up Parenting are indicated: 1) Confront, 2) Assess and 3) Remove. It's possible your child is building a model of the B-2 Bomber in the basement, but the glue supply should be on a scale with the project. Suspected VOC abuse requires medical and psychiatric assessment. All offending agents should be removed from the home. The good news is that most kids stop inhalants after one or two times.

However, some don't. Research has identified these risk factors for inhalant abuse:

- Conduct disorder
- History of cheating in school or stealing
- A family value system that does not object to drug use
- Kids who dislike school
- Kids with more emotionality
- Past history of using other drugs
- School expulsions and failures
- Criminal offenses
- Running away

Kids with these problems need care from multiple, coordinated professionals.

PCP and Ketamine

Tyrone's death from PCP resulted from drug induced psychotic behavior. A hallmark of PCP is that it causes psychotic violence. In a review of 104 PCP deaths in St. Louis, Missouri, eighty-one were from homicide, thirteen were suicides and six were from accidents. One third of all kids coming to an emergency room with PCP intoxication are likely to be violent. Ketamine is PCP's gentler sister. It's also called Special K, or simply K, on the street and has no relation to the popular cereal. The drug has clinical use in pediatric and veterinary settings as an anesthetic. A kid using ketamine is likely to have a source stealing the drug from a hospital or veterinary facility. K has a shorter life span in the brain than PCP and is less devastating. It may be eaten, snorted or injected. The latter carries with it the danger of HIV and hepatitis C. K is not likely to kill a kid by itself. Of eighty-seven ketamine-positive deaths in New York City from 1997–99, ketamine caused none when used exclusively.

The hallucinations, delusions and spaciness of PCP use resemble the symptoms of schizophrenia. Users take these drugs—no surprise here — to feel high. In the alphabet soup of drugs available at raves, kids can be taking K sold as "E," i.e., Ecstasy. Kids on K are high, grandiose, restless, anxious and confused. More serious troubles include chest pain and severe impairments in memory during toxicity. Memory problems can last several days after use. Recent research in England shows that in rats a high dose of PCP causes death of brain cells.

GHB, Not Quite a Prime Time Player

Jennifer, a jumpy computer programmer came to the emergency room of a local hospital. Twenty-six, attractive, articulate and educated, she worked in a competitive job market, but saw herself as shy. To meet men she went to clubs. To calm her nerves she took a drug a friend said would calm her nerves. It did. GHB (a.k.a. gamma-hydroxybutyrate) is an unapproved sedative which creates euphoria while melting away anxiety.

However, there is no free lunch in the drug world. Over time, she discovered that she couldn't start her day without GHB and then, she couldn't start it without doubling the dose. Her supply was gone within several weeks and so was her friend's supply. During Jennifer's first visit to the emergency room, she didn't mention taking GHB to the doctor who saw her. She was given an appointment to see a psychiatrist. During her second visit to the emergency room a few days later, she did mention her GHB use. By this time Jennifer was hearing her thoughts on television and seeing ants crawling over her skin. Her withdrawal delirium also brought with it visual and auditory hallucinations, sweating, nausea, vomiting, high blood pressure and agitation requiring restraints and sedation. It lasted eight days.

The club drug Jennifer took has been implicated in "date rapes" when drunk in doses of 0.5 to 4 g in alcohol or water. Alcohol and certain AIDS medications increase the effects of GHB, which can result in death. In the 1990s the Drug Enforcement Agency reported 5700 overdoses from this drug, along with sixty-five deaths, most often when GHB was used along with alcohol and narcotics.

Designer Drugs

Carbon, the stuff in charcoal briquettes and diamonds, is an atom that can chemically connect with four other atoms to give you stable 3-D structures. A single carbon atom can connect with many other kinds of atoms, including other carbon atoms, to give you a *gazillion different* molecules. Mother Nature tested out a lot of them over the last three billion years. The result? Perhaps fifty million species of living things, all holding together by virtue of the carbon-carbon bond.

Knowledge of carbon-carbon bonds can be used to make any kind of molecule, whether or not it is found in nature. Some folks have used this knowledge to make molecules to get people high. These inventions are called designer drugs. There is simply no practical limit to the number of combinations of carbon and other atoms that one can make in search of them. There is no way to completely prevent their invention, production or distribution. One chemist synthesized and tested in human volunteers at least 179 designer drugs for hallucinogenic property, which he optimistically called "tools for self-exposure." He tested the drugs on himself and then offered it to his wife and volunteers if "it hadn't caused a seizure." Ecstasy is a designer drug. DMT is another. These designer drugs are often referred to by an alphabet shorthand of organic chemistry and are made by modifying the structure of naturally occurring chemicals in the brain. It's easy to do and that means the designers are here to stay.

The underground chemist comes in different flavors: capitalist, scientist, therapist. Nearly always, however, the underground chemist is uninformed about the medical effects of his drugs. As a consequence, casualties litter the medical literature. The distribution of designer drugs is practicing medicine without a license on a grand scale.

As with other drugs, your role as a parent in the face of designer drugs is to: 1) educate your child, 2) confront your child about any unidentified substance in the home, 3) remove the substance from your home, 4) get laboratory testing of the substance and 5) have your child assessed medically, including a toxicology screen of his urine, if you notice mental change. Two caveats: 1) laboratory testing can be costly and 2) turning to local law enforcement agencies for help can backfire. The job of the police is to enforce the law, even if it means criminalizing your child's drug use. Only an enlightened police department will choose to get a kid drug help over criminally indicting him.

Exotic Plants

Over ninety plants are recognized worldwide for their ability to alter perception, thinking and emotion. When compared to chemically pure drugs, such as the designers described above, the drugs in these plants pose a less dangerous risk for kids, because they are consumed in doses thousands of times less potent than the chemically pure street varieties. Peyote and psilocybin mushrooms are considered exotics, even though any adventurous kid can grow mushrooms under his bed if he is so inclined.

On the other hand, this is *not* to say that any kid should feel free to eat any plant with impunity. As we discussed in chapter 1, certain plants work just fine as poisons, without the niceties of chemical purification. Wild mushrooms poison people every year. Nutmeg (yes, nutmeg), mace, morning glory seeds and wisteria are all poisonous in large enough doses. A basic rule for parents is that if it didn't come from a supermarket or the seed catalog, it's suspect until proven otherwise. Should you ban nutmeg from the spice rack? Of course not. However, revisit this question if your kid has already proven that she sees spice abuse as fair game for a Friday night. The following discussion only scratches the surface of available mind-altering botanicals and is intended to highlight those that are easily available, especially toxic or rising topics of medical interest.

Beyond the Spice Rack

Beyond the spice rack, where do kids get these exotics? They grow them or they buy them from the Internet. Air travel and the mail can make the exotic the ordinary. Thus, use by kids of drugs like Virola from the Amazon, Yopo from the Orinoco region or Shanín petunias from Ecuador is not unheard of today. One young man on the Internet describes cultivating a relationship with the South American vine Banisteriopsis. The excitement and pleasure is contagious in his report: "I have a wonderful friend growing in my living room or should I say taking over my living room…" This is also called Ayahuasca (caapi, pinde, natéma and yajé). Steeping the plant's bark produces a hallucinogenic drink. Plants like this vine have devotees on the internet whose web pages praise the plants' mental effects and direct viewers of any age to sources where they can be purchased. Once again, the mails and clandestine growers make police control of their use an ineffective social policy. Heads-up Parenting is the best defense against their abuse.

One of the oldest and more deadly hallucinogens, the mushroom Fly Agaric, also called Amanita, is thought to have been first discovered by Siberian hunters as they watched deer eat the mushroom and become intoxicated. This poisonous mushroom grows freely in the United States and Europe. Morning Glory seeds, another plant which can be found in a front yard near you, is a source of lysergic acid amide, which is 1/50th to 1/100th the strength of LSD. Nutmeg and mace in large doses can cause distortions in time and space, as well as feelings of detachment and hallucinations.

Deadly Nightshade

The deadly nightshade family of Europe and the datura families in Asia and the Americas include plants like the lowly jimson weed, thorn apple, mandrake, henbane, belladonna. The poisons in question are atropine, hyoscyamine and scopolamine, medically useful for anesthesia, motion sickness, diarrhea and as antidotes for nerve gas. Atropine and scopolamine are especially dangerous in kids. In overdose you can see dilated pupils, hot flushed skin, high fever, rapid heart, restlessness, confusion and disorientation. Death can occur from depressed breathing. Overdose either by plant or pure drug is plainly a medical emergency. Take any affected child to the nearest hospital where the appropriate antidotes and support measures can be given.

Iboga, the Most Significant African Hallucinogen

The main Iboga, a small shrub from Gabon, is ibogaine, a chemical similar to serotonin, the mother of all neurotransmitters. It has effects similar to Ecstasy, combining the effects of an hallucinogen with that of a stimulant. Deaths have been described from overdoses of this botanical preparation. Themes of death seem to occur often to individuals during the hallucinations it causes. This could be added to a future Surgeon General's warning.

There are claims that ibogaine is useful in the treatment of addictions to alcohol, amphetamines, cocaine and nicotine. Indeed, animals appear to reverse drug seeking behaviors following ibogaine pretreatment, perhaps following the dictum of once burnt, twice afraid. There is so far no well-controlled study in humans. Remember: the more extreme the claim, the less likely there is truth to it.

Take-Home Lesson #15

1) Junk drugs are not widespread problems but may be drugs of first choice for misinformed kids.

2) Do the "stink test" to know if your kid is fooling around with inhalants.
3) Nearly as many eight graders try inhalants as do marijuana, with far more depression and suicide as the result.
4) A drug is always more dangerous if injected. Needle = Major Red Flag.
5) In the face of your child using designer drugs: educate and confront your child, remove the substance from your home if you can and have your child medically assessed.

Part III

What to Do If Your Kid Is Already Using Drugs

Chapter 16

Tips for Parenting
the Friday Night Adventurer

Drug-using kids come in all flavors. Most are weekend adventurers, nibblers who experiment with legal or misdemeanor drugs like tobacco, pot and alcohol in small doses or infrequent intervals. The important things for parents to do are recognize drug use on this level and to step in before it gets out of control.

In many ways these kids are harder to reach than drug-dependent ones, since their experimentation has led to little or no trouble in school, with the law or, up until now, with their parents. So you have a hard sell in front of you. Tape the following list to the refrigerator door for a month. The kids will get the point.

The best result I have seen with this list is that it provokes the family into an honest discussion of drug use and consequences. Ideally, in discussion parents should cover the range from the academic (should dope be legalized?) to what the limits are for recreational drug use in the family. My limit and the one I suggest for your family is zero. No use. No permission to drink, smoke, use dope or whatever. There are very good reasons for my view and I want to share them with you:

Top 15 Reasons to Stay Off Drugs

15. Family conflict
14. School failure
13. Accidents
12. Brain injury
11. Psychosis
10. Job loss
 9. Impoverishment
 8. Depression
 7. Drug withdrawal
 6. Addiction
 5. Hepatitis C
 4. AIDS
 3. Prison
 2. Homicide
 1. Suicide

Outcomes for the Friday Night Adventurer, Confronted

Nothing is easy. So you pin up the *15 Reasons* and have a heart-to-heart talk with your child. What he does next is certain not to be what you wish for. Kids are much more creative than that. The Friday Night Adventurer may use drug use to provoke pandemonium. Hold onto your hat. You have read this book. At this point you know a lot about drugs and what they can do to kids.

Wish vs. Reality

Your kid takes what you said totally seriously and never takes another drink or drug until he is forty-five. This is possible, but highly unlikely. Another alternative is your kid takes what you said seriously, but concludes a little dope on Friday nights won't kill her. When she comes home from a party, she smells like smoke. You can choose to ignore this regression, but only at your kid's peril. Instead of the parent's ostrich maneuver (you will notice it is opposite to the Heads-up position), engage the kid right off, along the lines of the discussion in chapter 6.

Setting a zero tolerance limit means reinforcing what you say with action. Limits have to be proportionate to the offense. A light touch is recommended, but one that will stick out in a kid's memory.

If you suspect your child has returned to being a Friday night adventurer, you need evidence. Positive urine tests for cannabinols, which can be obtained by a visit to the pediatrician or local laboratory, are good. So are finding smoking paraphernalia like papers and pipes and of course, dope itself. Open admissions of use are best, if you don't get them under duress. They're especially good, because they establish a certain level of honesty between parent and child, which is precious. Any kid who admits using dope again to a parent deserves commendation for honesty, not punishment, the first time around.

However, if and when the drug use goes on, you must turn to the iron hand. Well, maybe just the plastic hand. Something to get the kid's attention besides a tantrum. A combination of steps can help, like drug education at home or school, frequent parent-kid check-ins, home grounding for weekends or weeks and bearing more chores at home or volunteer work in the community. The extent to which your kid can get with this program is the extent to which he will be able to stay out of the darker levels of drug experimentation, the next one being hardcore adventuring.

Hardcore Drug Adventuring

The kid who persists in using weekend alcohol and/or pot and advances to LSD or Ecstasy has reached a more dangerous level. This is risk taking on a bigger scale. A firmer hand is needed for these kids. The key principle is employ the least restrictive form of intervention to do the job.

For a kid at this level of use, I suggest:

- **Formal drug education.** There are many places in the typical community where this can occur. If your kid is busted for a misdemeanor and sentenced to a state run alcohol education course, don't resist it. It'll be an eye opener for the whole family. After school, evening or weekend drug programs for kids abound. Contact a local guidance counselor.
- **Community service.** Ten or twenty hours of volunteer work at a local nursing home, shelter or kids' club will do more

good things for a kid than you can imagine. It's important for kids to realize that they have skills that people actually value.

- **Religion.** Remember, it reduces the risk of drug use in kids according to statistics. Most churches and temples have programs for kids of all ages. Make her go six times ("to see if you like it"). In that time bonding may occur between your kid and others to make the activity a steady event.

- **Support your kid's interests**. Actively. Chauffeur her to the ball game across town or pay for guitar lessons. Nurture the good dreams of your children. Positive reinforcement works.

- **Assess your kid's liabilities candidly.** This is especially true for academic weaknesses. Schools cannot begin to address all of the unique learning styles, disabilities and behavior problems they see each day. Engage an educational specialist to help you map out strategies to solve the problem.

- **Get a psychological assessment.** This step is especially important if the child has developed persistent weekend use of drugs. A psychiatric assessment is a good idea to handle or rule out other problems that may lurk in the background. Drug counseling individually and in groups can help here, too.

The Good Therapist

She is patient, kind, experienced. He is knowledgeable about drugs and psychiatric diagnoses. She is on a first name basis with the school counselors in the community. He is highly recommended and credited with saving the lives of dozens of the neighbors' kids. She answers the telephone, returns calls and periodically invites parents to check in. He builds trust and respects confidentiality, but will actively intervene in a crisis. The good news is that although I've never met a person who imbues all these qualities, I have known therapists who come darn close.

For talk therapy, I have found that the differences in competence between psychiatrists, psychologists and social workers often are indistinguishable. For Double Trouble kids, who need assessment and treatment of specific mental illness in addition to drug problems, a psychiatrist is needed. For a kid who is a hardcore adventurer, a savvy drug counselor who is part of a teen drug program may be able to reach the child, speak his language and work with him. Teenaged drug abusers do not thrive on subtlety. The motto on the wall of one treatment center boiled it down nicely for the kids: "Change or die."

I support a try 'em before you buy 'em philosophy, at least for the long haul. Ask the child to see the therapist for several visits. If the child begins to open up during these sessions, you've found a match. If not, you probably have to look further. A compromise with the help-rejecting kid is to negotiate a fixed number of visits, e.g., six, to see if the therapist and child have rapport and are making progress. Don't look for a miraculous turnabout in your child after a visit or two. It probably took many years for the problems to develop. Be patient with the therapist, and the kid, as they work at putting things back together. Make sure the therapist is available to meet with the family from time to time, to reassure your family the kid is not as bad off as you think and that things are not as good as he claims.

Finding a good therapist isn't easy. Engaging a truculent teen in therapy requires a level of clinical skill approaching magic. Do not take lightly a bond that grows between a teen and a therapist. It's precious and providing the treatment is going in the right direction, you should protect it. There are many good things that can come from such a relationship. Reaching a place where a kid is no longer a drug abuser, of course, is the most important.

Drug Testing and the Heads-up Parent

When Lindsay Earls, a sixteen-year-old member of the high school's choir, band and an honor student, was asked to provide urine for a drug test at school, she refused. She was a good kid, she felt. She did not use drugs. There was no reason to invade her privacy. She took her case to the Supreme Court, where her attorneys argued that such testing violated the Fourth Amendment which protects American citizens from unreasonable searches and seizures.

Not so, Justice Thomas argued in a 5 to 4 decision. Schools have a greater interest in protecting children than in maintaining privacy. Besides, Justice Thomas argued, kids don't have the same privacy rights as adults. But four of the Justices saw the case differently. Dissenting Justice Ginsburg wrote, in reference to the school's desire to drug test kids involved in Future Homemakers of America, Future Farmers of America and the marching band, that "Notwithstanding nightmarish images of out-of-control flatware, livestock run amok and colliding tubas disturbing the peace and quiet of the school, most students are engaged in activities that are not safety sensitive in an unusual degree." She concluded, "The school's policy thus falls short doubly if deterrence is its aim: It invades the privacy of students who need deterrence least, and risks steering students at greatest risk for substance abuse away from extracurricular activities that potentially may palliate drugs problems," echoing a position taken by the National Educational Association and the American Academy of Pediatrics.

In the name of the drug war, kids in public high schools have been placed in the position of being treated as guilty until they are proven innocent. Worse, kids struggling with drugs will be inclined to avoid those very school programs that can help them back on the road to productivity. So what's a Heads-up Parent to do about drug testing? Here are some clarifying principles I believe are important:

- First, if there is a *suspicion* a kid is using drugs, there is likely to be little argument from Ruth Ginsburg or any other justice that there *may be* a place for drug testing the kid. But at home, the Heads-up Parent rarely needs to resort to such a measure. The quickest drug test for the two commonest drugs is the hug-and-inhale screen for alcohol and marijuana. The results are in much faster than from urine screens.
- Second, asking a kid what he's up to can open up a dialogue that in the long run is life saving.
- For a kid sinking into serious drug problems, the problems will identify themselves. A kid with poor gait or slurred speech doesn't need a drug test. He needs to be taken to an emergency room.
- Despite the Supreme Court's decisions on the Fourth Amendment in recent years, kids deserve to be treated with dignity and respect in the courts. That includes a gradually increasing right of privacy.

- Despite a kid's claim for the right of privacy, *if there is a suspicion,* a parent must set aside privacy rights in favor of safety. This can mean searching a kid's room for drugs, seizing them and finding out what is going on.

The Federal Office of National Drug Control Policy in 2002 published a guide for parents, *What You Need to Know About Drug Testing in School.* The Guide adopts the sensible tone of recognizing the important role of parents and communities in deciding such actions about their kids. But the ONDCP stumbles with its claim that "testing has been shown to be extremely effective at reducing drug use in schools and businesses." This is simply not what the data have shown in schools so far. Ryoko Yamaguchi and his collaborators at the University of Michigan in 2003 surveyed 722 secondary schools for four years and found no differences in drug abuse between schools that had drug testing and those that didn't.

The Twelve Golden Rules for Parents of Drug Adventurers

Let's streamline our discussion of intervening when your kid is a drug adventurer into the Twelve Golden Rules for Parents of Drug Adventurers, which follow. Begin the job by looking in the mirror. If you don't like what you see, change it: get rid of the drugs and booze in your life—if they are there in the first place. Think more and judge less. Take the judge out of judgmental.

Then take a good, lingering look at your kids. If you don't like what you see, try to change it. Remember, you can't control their lives the way you used to when they were small. They still need you, but they are becoming independent adults. Some things you can change and some…well, you can't. But the major thing is to try when you see destructive behavior.

Take-Home Lesson #16

1) Make your home a drug-free zone.
2) Stay clean of drugs yourself.
3) Support your kid's strengths.
4) Keep your child in school.

5) Keep an eye on your kid's friendships.
6) Involve your kid in religion or formal ethical education.
7) Get your kid involved in community activity.
8) Listen to what he is saying.
9) Tell her what you're thinking.
10) Set limits.
11) Make a contract.
12) Keep your perspective.

Chapter 17

How to Manage an Overdose

If you are turning to this chapter, because you think your child has just overdosed on drugs, put this book in your car and take her to the nearest hospital. Do it now.

Go directly to the emergency room. Do not seek the world's best emergency room, but the nearest. Time is essential in countering overdoses, not great hands, brains or proton accelerators. Your head will race with many reasons why you think you shouldn't take her to an emergency room. Be aware that over 325,000 kids and young adults in 2000 were treated for drug overdoses. Here are a few common mistakes that parents make when faced with an overdosing child:

- You fear that your kid will be prosecuted and/or get an arrest record and so delay treatment.
- You think of trying a home remedy for overdoses you heard about.
- You don't want to upset your kid, who tells you through the haze of an overdose that "everything is all right."
- You believe your child is only asleep, clutching that empty pill bottle for security and will awaken momentarily.

- You believe your kid is "just dead drunk."
- You think your HMO will not pay for overdoses without prior authorization.

These are not reasons to delay. Take the kid to an emergency room now. Why? Because an OD is a toxic chemical crisis requiring specialized care. You and your child can work on solving all of the other problems later, but only if your child's not dead. Take with you the bottles of every pill to which she might have had access, along with verbal reports from any friends who were using with her. Lives have been saved simply because a roommate or friend said a single word to the emergency room doctor.

I am not implying that the situation you face will be easy. It will be one of the most difficult things you've ever done, sitting in one of those uncomfortable plastic chairs while your child is whisked away on a gurney. You'll be there for hours. They'll probably be doing a lot of tests, managing her fluids, electrolytes, toxic effects of the drugs. Maybe a longer hospitalization will be required. Some parents flip dully through the old magazines strewn around. Others just sit looking up anxiously every time an orderly in a white coat walks through a swinging door. This is a good definition of Parent Hell.

If you have a copy of this book in the car, go get it. Use this book to manage the people and events which go along with treating an overdosing child. I know you're probably dazed and depressed, however, action pays. Believe it or not, this is a major opportunity for your child to turn a life-saving corner. In the game of basketball, helping a teammate score a goal is referred to as an *assist*. Taking action now when your kid is at his lowest point can be one of the more important assists in his and your life.

Emergency Jumpstart to Treatment

When your child is on a gurney, with the fluids dripping from an intravenous hookup and the blood tests cooking, it's safe to conclude on some level from inside her drug-disordered brain she is saying, "Help me, Mom. Help me, Dad." Seize the day.

The special opportunity you have, once your kid is out of the acute medical danger of the overdose, is to help her jump-start into treatment. An OD is a tough way to start the road to recovery, but consider the alternatives: prostitution, homelessness, jail, AIDS and death. After your child has been given emergency treatment for the overdose, she will either be treated entirely in the emergency room or admitted to the intensive care unit.

Things to Do if Your Child is Treated Solely in the Emergency Room

Fortunately, the chances are low that your child will be admitted to the Intensive Care Unit. That means that all the critical decisions regarding her treatment for drug use will be made by the emergency room staff. Make yourself an active part of the process:

- Request that a **mental health professional** see your child then and there in the ER before she is discharged. The consultant professional preferably should be versed in the ways of substance abusers. If a professional such as this is not available in this hospital, ask for a list of those who are available elsewhere
- With your kid's permission, sit in on the **interview**. Your child's brain may not be as clear as yours at this moment. If your child is given to shame and guilt and the consultant asks you to leave in the middle of the interview, do so gracefully. Your presence there can inhibit as much as facilitate. If this person doesn't connect with your child or seems very inexperienced, look for someone else. Don't expect miracles from this initial session.
- Do not leave the emergency department without assurance that a psychiatric assessment for **suicide** was performed. Not all ODs are in the name of fun. Suicide is a real problem in kids and drugs are a major contributory factor. Insist that the emergency room staff rule out that your kid is acutely suicidal. They can't rule out whether your child is chronically suicidal. That is, they can't answer the question of whether your child will attempt suicide in the distant future. No one can tell you that. But it's their job to make the call on whether your kid is safe to go home with you that night or needs to be hospitalized.

- Ask the emergency room doctor if your child needs admission to a **detox program**. Detoxification programs do two main things: they intervene during life threatening withdrawals from drugs; and they serve as valuable bridges from (brief) inpatient to (long term) outpatient treatment. Detoxing children is a lesser clinical need than addressing the multiple dimensions of kids in trouble, though older teens may need detoxification help as their drug illness progresses. The emergency room physician is most certainly capable of recognizing an impending dangerous drug withdrawal.

- Ask the emergency room doctor whether admission to a children's (or adults') **psychiatric service** is needed. Often, but not always, a kid is admitted to a psychiatric service for suicidal or psychotic disorders. Destructive or self-destructive behavior is often a good indication for a hospital stay. Such stays in the era of managed costs are brief. Most important is the effort the hospital will put into care after discharge. In the battle for sobriety, that's what is most important.

- Don't leave the emergency room without **a follow-up appointment** for a drug focused outpatient psychological assessment, if at all possible. If it is three in the morning (and it usually is), then get phone numbers of two programs that work with kids and start calling first thing in the morning. I suggest two because chances are at least one of them will be busy, their answering machine will be on, the phone will be answered by someone who writes down your phone number with six digits, the waiting list will be jammed and intake will be booking dates sometime after your child's forty-fifth birthday. Get phone numbers if an appointment can't be made at that moment. Make the calls. Take the child to the appointment. It is not possible to put a comprehensive treatment plan into place in an emergency room. Don't ask for the moon.

What to Do If Your Kid Is Admitted to the ICU

If your child is admitted to the Intensive Care Unit of the hospital, rather than being treated entirely in the emergency room, it is likely that her doctors are concerned that her life is endangered or, at the least, she needs her basic systems of heart and lungs to be stabilized. Specialized medications or procedures may be needed. This is routine for the ICU staff. It is a nightmare for parents. Please don't be paralyzed with fear. You must try to be proactive. Ask a lot of questions. Make lists of them before you meet with your kid's doctors. Identify a key player, preferably the child's own pediatrician or internist, with whom you can communicate for daily updates.

Expect doctors to rotate through the service several times a day. Even doctors go home to sleep. Get as physically close to the bedside as is permitted for as long as you and your spouse can. Report changes in your child's breathing rate, cardiac monitor and mental status to the nursing staff as they happen. Identify the nurses on each shift assigned to your child. They're the point people. Use them to educate you about what's going on. Educate them, too, about changes you perceive in your child's condition. Make yourself a volunteer member of the team. Not all nursing staff will welcome you. Tough. It's your kid, not theirs. Just don't get in their way. The staff generally know what they're doing. Your added input can help. As your child's discharge day nears, request:

- A psychiatric assessment. Is she suicidal? Psychotic? A danger to herself if she is released home?
- Should she be hospitalized psychiatrically? The majority of kids who end up in ICUs after overdoses are often candidates for psychiatric hospitalization. If one is recommended, accept the recommendation. It may well become the crucial stepping stone for your child's recovery from drug use.
- If your child is not a candidate for psychiatric hospitalization, insist on a referral to an aftercare program to deal with her drug issue.
- Make these same requests even if your child does not end up in the ICU.

Whatever the consequences of treating your child's overdose, through the emergency room or intensive care treatment, be comforted that you have done the right things. Without treatment, your child may have died. With it, he may get on the road to recovery.

Take-Home Lesson #17

1) If you see the slightest signs your child has taken a drug over-dose, take her to the nearest emergency room.
2) Take this book with you and use it to manage the necessary steps you must take.
3) Despite your fears, accept that this emergency may be the opportunity to jump-start treatment.
4) Once your child is medically clear, insist on a mental health assessment of his condition for safety.
5) Get a referral to the appropriate treatment resource then and there.

Chapter 18

When Kids Are Addicts

Addiction is a dark passage of the soul. When it afflicts a child, it tears at a parent in the same way that the child being afflicted by any other life-threatening disease does. Addiction, however, is unlike other illnesses, because when *addict* is the label, blaming the victim often follows. It also does not start like other illnesses. Parents of an addicted child see no explosive fever or seizure, as they would if their child had meningitis or a brain tumor. More often, a parent describes the history of a kid who, at first, only casually experimented with alcohol or pills. Then the child insidiously turned into someone else, with problems in school, changes in personality and, eventually, medical ill effects. Other times parents are caught completely unawares and numbed into inactivity, when they learn that their kid has stumbled into addiction. With either path, finding out you have an addicted child brings with it depression, fear, anxiety and shame.

Death occurs only rarely in adolescent addiction, at least in the early stages of drug abuse. Deterioration is more common, as the victim is encircled by the drug life and its consequences. When most parents of addicted children grieve, it is for the loss of dreams they once had for these children, replaced now with fears for those children who are physically ill, emotionally impaired and commit unspeakable acts to feed their habits. Too often parents, caught in webs of guilt, deprive themselves of the comfort of friends and access to compassionate medical care. And so they too are condemned without relief to join their children in the seemingly endless cycle of recoveries and relapses that is further torture.

It is easy to forget when you are caught up in this cycle of chaos that an addicted kid suffers from a drug-damaged brain. As the Spanish scientists Jordi Cami and Magi Farré wrote in the *New England Journal of Medicine* in 2004, "continued use induces adaptive changes in the central nervous system that lead to tolerance, physical dependence, sensitization, craving and relapse." They could have been talking about Leigh.

Addiction's Downward Spiral

Leigh was one of those kids who was both bright and learning disabled. The son of white-collar parents, his reading difficulty went unrecognized throughout elementary school. So did his abuse of pot and then pain medications in high school. When Leigh dropped out of the community college, his father, Fred, a draftsman, who had dropped out years before himself, was not surprised. Neither was Leigh's mother when she found pot in his room. Fred still used marijuana and alcohol to unwind each night after work.

Once out of school, Leigh couldn't keep a job. He overslept. His mother called him lazy. But she dropped the lazy theory the morning she saw telltale tracks of needle marks on his arms. Leigh was shooting heroin, he admitted, and had a six to ten bag a day habit. His parents did the right thing: they took him to a drug clinic for treatment. However, Leigh didn't keep his appointments. He was either too high or too sick from drug withdrawals. Instead, he prowled the streets for any drug that would take away his nausea and melt away his pain.

After he withdrew cash from his mother's credit card to buy dope, his parents threw him out. Chastened, he returned home weeks later, promising to stay in treatment. But shortly thereafter, he pawned his mother's engagement ring and bought OxyContin with the money. His parents threw him out again. Over the years, Leigh cycled in and out of detoxification and rehabilitation programs. One night, against the wall of a warehouse, he shot a combination of OxyContin and heroin into one of few remaining veins available to his needle and drifted away. The medical examiner ruled Leigh's death a suicide. His parents called it an accident. He was twenty-four.

Where Does the Parent of an Addict Start?

The suffering of Leigh and his parents was immense. Addicted early, he hadn't developed the skills to fight back against his habit. His parents were helpless to get him to do anything. The result was death for Leigh and decades of sadness, rage and guilt for his parents.

It doesn't have to end that way. The challenges to parents whose child is an addict are twofold. You must help that child as much as you can and you must protect yourself and others in your family from being consumed by the experience. Start your child's recovery process with conventional therapies, not the lunatic fringe. Turn to treatments in the least restrictive environments (outpatient, not inpatient) that the clinical condition of your kid requires and ratchet them up to more controlled (and, alas, expensive) environments as needed. Treatments beyond outpatient clinics that work for addicts include:

- Self-help groups
- Day hospitals
- Evening programs
- Inpatient hospital stays
- Residential treatment
- Relocation treatment

As I talk about in chapter 19, a large percentage of kids in trouble with drugs have other psychiatric troubles, too. Parents of drug users need to learn how to "see double." Kids who relapse multiple times need residential treatment.

Self-help Groups

Alcoholics Anonymous is a very good self-help group. The advan-
tages of AA are that it's down to earth, tough-minded, direct,
diverse, spiritual, supportive, free and effective. Before you sign
your kid up, though, be aware of its limitations. It's adult oriented
and not useful for young teens. It's spiritual, a definite liability if
your kid's idea of a Higher Power is only a bigger dealer. AA views
vary meeting to meeting, but it generally has a non-medical view of
addiction that often talks down the use of medication for psychiatric illnesses — a point of view that is disastrous for kids with, e.g.,
schizophrenia or depression. In addition, AA does not always deal
well with forms of addiction other than alcohol. Similarly struc-
tured self-help groups are available for narcotics (NA) and cocaine
(CA).

All of these programs are based on a traditional Twelve Step
structure. Phone any local AA office or find out how they function on
the web at: *http://www.aa.org/*. The Twelve Steps are a terrific map
from addiction to recovery, beginning with the state of helplessness
the addict feels, the involvement of a Higher Power, the making of
amends for past hurts and the reaching out to other addicts in need.
Embedded within the AA program is a crucial bit of wisdom that
likely makes neurobiological sense. The part of the addict's brain that
sends drug-seeking demands to the rest of the brain does it every day.
To combat this, the AA meeting immunizes an addict against relapse.
But in early recovery, *it's only good for one day*. Hence, the value in
advising an addict in recovery to go to "90 meetings in 90 days." This
is particularly helpful, since the greatest number of relapses occur
within the first three months after cleaning up. Staying clean requires
skills and skills take time to develop. Patience is needed all around a
kid in recovery.

Day Hospitals and Evening Programs

In these programs, your kid goes to school during the day at the hospital and learns how to get sober. Or the kid goes to school during
the day and goes to the program at night. This is a terrific idea. It is
vastly less expensive than overnight hospitalizations and residential
care. On the spectrum of restricting a kid's movements, day programs

occupy a spot between outpatient and residential treatments. Day programs keep the child in the family and a natural environment which allows her to practice healthy alternatives and coping skills. There is a paradox in this. One can argue that allowing a kid in early recovery back into the environment where she is likely to be exposed to drugs is like telling her to march while tying her shoelaces together. However, the next morning after a relapse, she will find herself in the day program again, where kids learn to drop their denial and build their drug refusal skills. Programs often invite the family in to participate in the recovery. Psychiatric services are usually available to get at other illnesses that are present. Unfortunately, some insurance companies have resisted paying for this beneficial and economic treatment.

Many kids have a sense of invulnerability, self-centeredness and an all-or-nothing worldview. A good treatment program knows what makes (many) adolescents tick: role models, imitation, peer pressure, action and immediate gratification.

There are few day programs completely dedicated to kids. Instead, youthful addicts are treated with adults, which is at best a compromise. Second, an old engineering principle applies to helping a kid recover from addiction. In any job, you can ask for fast, good or cheap. But you only get to pick two. And in the treatment of addictions, fast is rare indeed.

Inpatient Hospitalizations

When hospitalization is needed for an addicted child, the longer, the better. Unfortunately, in the era of managed care, long stays are seldom possible. Worse is that even fewer inpatient programs deal exclusively with adolescents. 20 percent of all patients in drug treatment are under the age of nineteen, but only 5 percent of all programs have adolescents as the focus. Nevertheless, much can be accomplished even in a short stay on an adult unit. Goals for hospitalization:

- Safe withdrawal from an addictive agent (alcohol, cocaine, narcotics, anti-anxiety drugs)
- Physical examination, especially for signs of infection
- Routine tests for liver and kidney function and nutrition
- Pregnancy test for sexually active girls
- Random urine screens for drugs

- Screening tests for HIV and hepatitis
- Steady surveillance for drugs and their use
- Psychiatric evaluation to identify other treatable problems with the appropriate use of psychiatric medicines when necessary
- Group therapy focused on relapse prevention and learning social skills (anger management, assertiveness, communication)
- Family therapy focused on ending enabling behaviors, resolving interpersonal conflicts and involving other family members with psychopathology
- Restrictions imposed on the addict's social interactions, visitors and smoking
- Seamless transition to an aftercare treatment plan

A hospital is not a rest home. The more areas covered, the better the program. Crucial to the goals discussed is the last one: transition. Your child is likely to be in the hospital only for a short time. What happens after discharge will make or break his recovery. Key points to look for in an aftercare plan:

- An appointment in hand *before* your child leaves the hospital
- Referral to a day or evening program
- Referral to an experienced drug counselor
- Opportunity for continued family therapy
- Connection with a psychiatrist for finding and treating conditions which the child may have been trying to self-medicate on his own
- Proper use of diagnostic helpers such as breath and urine screens
- School involvement
- Connection with other recovery groups, preferably ones with other kids

Residential Treatment

These programs tend to fall into two groups: publicly funded ones and private ones. The former have more customers than they know what to do with. This is the result of a genuine epidemic in addictions and a woeful shortage of public funding for residential care. Repeated failures at outpatient and day program treatment facilities are the usual indication for admission. Another sensible requirement is that the patient come to the treatment setting free of all abused drugs. This usually means that a kid is first admitted to a psychiatric inpatient setting, detoxed and then transferred directly to the residence with no stops along the way. Never forget that a drug detoxification is only a short-term treatment. It does not by itself succeed in a few days to teach everything a kid needs to know to resist drugs and avoid relapse. A kid fresh from detox can easily slip back into addition. Hence the absolute necessity of post-hospital care.

Private residential treatment is usually hospitals which provide a range of services, the first of which is a twenty-eight-day inpatient program. Sandra Bullock lived in one in the Hollywood film, *28 Days*, a superb rendition of patients in early recovery. (I give this film two thumbs up, despite the idyllic horse stables, ponds and famous athletes for patients). Many managed care companies consider these twenty-eight-day Minnesota-model programs the dinosaurs of addiction care. Nothing could be farther from the truth. They tend to be for chemically dependent adults. They are based on the AA belief that change is possible; the goal is abstinence and changes in life style.

Residential treatment is the last in a line of progressively restrictive environments. They are not for everyone, but for addicts who have tried without success multiple times through inpatient hospitalizations to clean up and stay clean. They actually work, not 100 percent and not forever. (*Addiction* is forever. *Recovery* is only as long as the patient chooses to make it.) They don't all cost $15,000 a month. Some programs, such as the Betty Ford Center, provide scholarships. And most important, residential programs offer what the addict needs the most: a long period of time away from drugs and dedicated to learning the business of sobriety. Longer is better.

Another way of reaching this goal is by living in a halfway house. This concept has become quite popular in the last decade. The drill is that an addict cleans up in a hospital and then is transferred without her feet touching the street directly to a halfway house. There she stays for up to six months, living in a community of others who are also in recovery. Limits are set. Lessons are taught. Medical care is attended to. Often the staff of such programs consists to a large extent of addicts in extended recovery.

Thus, professionalism is not always in abundance and not all halfway houses are equal. But when they are good, they help and the work they do is priceless.

Self and Other Cures

Luke was addicted to heroin within weeks after his teenage band made it to the medium time, releasing their first CD and opening the road show of a big time band. Luke's band fell apart about a year later when all the members came down with hepatitis B. His life fell apart about a year after that. He failed to kick the habit despite multiple tries in inpatient detox programs. His father offered to pay for a twenty-eight day rehab program, but Luke felt that it was a sacrifice of which he was unwilling to take advantage. Instead, he moved with his drug free girlfriend, Natalie, from the city of his addiction to a farm setting in Kansas. The second day there, Luke promptly went into withdrawal without medical help, but never looked back. In the months that followed, the young couple settled into a life of carpentry and homemaking. They had children. Luke has been sober for the past ten years.

By moving to a distant state and giving himself a fresh start, Luke cured himself. Drug addiction is a highly conditioned set of behavioral responses to the environment. Getting a person out of that environment can do him a world of good. No harmful stimulus means no harmful response.

Golden Rules

If you are new to the world of addiction, you will be dismayed to hear that it usually takes an addict multiple attempts to put together the elements of recovery. How many detoxes does it take to stay clean? As many as needed to get the job done. A fall back then becomes drug free days — the more, the better. Like heart disease, cancer and depression, addiction evolves in a pattern of remissions and relapses. Hope for a cure, but expect and plan for, a relapse.

The one area where parents seem to have the most trouble is understanding and resisting the temptation to *enable their kid to use drugs*. Enabling is a funny concept. You do it without knowing it. Here are some examples of enabling:

- The dad who gives his kid a ritualistic sip of his beer every night
- The mom who smells pot in her kid's bedroom and says nothing
- The guilt-ridden divorced parent who continues an allowance to his son despite having found the son's cocaine paraphernalia
- The parents who pay their addicted kid's rent even when they know the money is being used to buy drugs

Enabling often begins when a parent denies a problem exists and then commits acts which keep it happening. Guilt plays a role. Addicted kids are masters of manipulation ("If you don't send me the check, I'll starve!") And money is a key way to enable a kid to use drugs, but enabling can occur just as easily by supplying your kid with money equivalents. It's really easy to do and really hard to admit to yourself you're doing it.

The job of parenting an addicted kid is enormous. It can go on for years. And worse, although Heads-up Parenting can help, you can't do it if your kid refuses to be part of the program. Nevertheless, stop enabling, stick with Heads-up Parenting, but remember that your home is not a drug treatment facility. You can take her to a facility, if she's willing. If she isn't, try again later. Don't drive yourself crazy if you are not successful. Stay empathic and connected, but don't allow one kid's illness to sicken the rest of the family. Protect yourself and your family from drug driven predations. Avoid enabling the addiction with gifts, loans and credit cards that can be converted into drugs. Don't neglect trying to get the kid treatment for other psychiatric illnesses.

Remember that whatever terrible times this illness has in store for you and your family, you are not the first person on Earth to have gone through them. You can find a raft of insight, advice and love simply by attending an Al-Anon or another group's meeting. Al-Anon, like AA, respects the anonymity of its membership, but its mission is to support the families of the problem drinker. Nar-Anon provides a similar service for the families of other types of addiction. One of the more powerful positive therapeutic experiences parents can have is discovering that they are not alone.

There are only a handful of principles you need to keep in mind to make the best of a terrible situation. I call them the *Golden Rules for the Parents of Addicts* and they comprise this chapter's take-home lesson. The most important: Don't give up. Hope is your greatest weapon. Hold onto it. Spread it around. In your bleakest moment, think of a time when your child was bright-eyed, clear-headed and there was laughter in the air. Then have faith. Such a time can come again.

Take-Home Lesson #18

1) Stay empathic.
2) Stay connected.
3) Be creative.
4) Be aware that addiction makes honest kids liars. Sobriety does the opposite.
5) Set limits to protect your family.
6) Detox kids under medical supervision.
7) Look for addicted kids' underlying psychiatric problems.
8) Plan your response to relapse before it happens.
9) Don't let your home become a drug treatment facility.
10) Don't enable.
11) Get help and support for yourself.
12) Don't give up.

Chapter 19

Double Trouble:
The Dually Diagnosed Kid

Nine out of ten kids abusing drugs are burdened with secondary psychiatric diagnoses. These are Double Trouble kids. Besides help with drug problems, they need special help with mental illness. This chapter discusses how drug abuse is linked to mental illness and how you can recognize Double Trouble kids. Before a scintilla of treatment is contemplated, clear-headed diagnosis is needed.

Again, do not rush. The power of good diagnosis is that it implies specific treatment, but if the diagnosis is wrong, chances are treatment will be wrong, too. And in Double Trouble kids, diagnosis can be very difficult for a number of reasons. A kid's mental state may be too clouded by her drug of choice to reveal her underlying emotional problems, which is a poor time to assess a chronic depression or anxiety disorder.

Leroy, one of my patients with underlying depression, began to show problems when his grades began to slip in the eighth grade. In the eleventh grade, he entered a teen psychiatric service following arrest for possession of over an ounce of marijuana. Only after cleaning up from the drug for several months, documented by negative urine screens, did it become clear that Leroy was suffering from a significant depression which predated his drug use by several years. When he finally was started on an antidepressant, he remarked, "It's like somebody turned the lights on."

Mental illnesses also can be caused by drugs. Alcohol, for example, can cause depression. But a drinking kid can also get depressed because of head trauma, a personality problem, chemical imbalances or the fact that he has just been suspended from school or been jilted by his girlfriend. Whatever the reason, sorting all these possibilities out is the job for a professional.

Ideally, a kid should be free of all drugs for a month before a diagnosis of mental condition is attempted. This introduces us to one of the tougher dilemmas in treating Double Troubles. Should we withhold antidepressant medication for a month from a kid who is drug involved and actively suicidal? My answer is no. Suicidal behavior must be addressed. This means mandatory hospitalization, which also means drug detox. Clinical judgment dictates whether an antidepressant or other medication is needed or if the kid's depression is expected to clear when he cleans up. To make such critical judgments, you need professionals.

The Value of Seeing Double

Heads-up Parenting means that you know how to see double if you have to, when it comes to a kid who is messing with drugs. Drug abuse increases the risk for certain psychiatric illnesses compared to the rates in non-drug users. Drug users are at greater risk for:

- Depression (the risk is doubled)
- Panic attacks (the risk is tripled)
- Schizophrenia (the risk goes up five times)
- Bipolar disorder (the risk goes up seven times)

The most likely diagnosis with a drug using kid is depression. But there's more. Kids with conduct and personality disorders are more often mixed up with drugs and vice versa. Kids with attention deficit hyperactivity disorder (ADHD) can get into drug trouble. Ironically, they often benefit from attention focusing drugs like Ritalin and Adderall, which carry with them abuse potential. Treatment of ADHD is not without risk, but it is effective. Close monitoring by parents and professionals alike is the answer to this dilemma.

The Great Debate

Which comes first, drug use or psychiatric illness? That is, are drugs the result of mental illness or the cause? Some experts argue that kids turn to drugs for self-medication. We know that kids who are victims of physical and sexual abuse often turn to drugs in later life. In our own research, we found that cocaine addicts with depression suffered depression years before cocaine was in the picture.

On the other hand, drug use can be a blow from which not all kids bounce back equally. Alcohol is widely known as a "depressant." Studies show that kids with schizophrenia who abuse drugs have significantly more difficulty in daily life than schizophrenic kids who don't. One study done in Los Angeles by Andrew Shaner and his colleagues found that schizophrenic patients who were into cocaine had more hospital admissions for psychotic symptoms at the beginning of each month, shortly after receiving disability payments which were diverted to coke. This team raised the disturbing question of whether this pattern represented a revolving door.

Katie's story illustrates the interplay between drug use and other psychiatric illness more clearly. Her mother called her Little Miss Sunshine in her younger years. In high school Katie was recognized for her expressive artwork. Her dream was to go to art school and learn how to paint with oils. When a friend told her that tripping on LSD would "make her more creative," she held off until the night of her junior prom. Then, after the shouting and dancing, she dropped acid for the first time. In the next few months, she tried the drug three more times. She told herself the added trips were clearing up the confusion of her first trip. However, the voices and delusions she began to experience told her otherwise. What followed in the next decade were a series of crippling psychotic breaks and hospitalizations for schizophrenia.

What pushed Katie over the edge of reality? Certainly LSD played a part. Would she have suffered her illness if she hadn't tripped? I don't believe so, but no one can be sure. People suffered schizophrenia centuries before the discovery of LSD. On the other hand, LSD users interviewed in an outpatient psychiatric clinic suffered twice as much psychosis as non-users. Perhaps another study illustrates best the dilemmas of the Great Debate. Stephen Gilman at Harvard and I asked if depression led to alcoholism or vice versa. The answer, to our surprise, was yes and yes, each increased the risk for the other.

Do Drugs Lead To Psychiatric Illness?

Table 11 summarizes what we know about psychiatric illnesses which are known to follow drug use. It's organized by specific drugs listed in a column on the left. Across the top is a list of various psychiatric diagnoses. A Danger Sign marks when a specific drug can lead to a certain diagnosis. For example, let's look at alcohol. Alcohol, as I've indicated before, is tied to depression, psychosis, panic and cognitive disorders. Other drugs have their own effects.

TABLE 11: Drugs and Psychiatric Illness

	Depression	Pyschosis	Panic	HPPD	Cognitive Disorders
Alcohol	YES	YES	YES		YES
LSD	YES	YES	YES	YES	
Marijuana	YES	YES	YES	YES	
Stimulants	YES	YES	YES		
Sedatives	YES		YES		YES
PCP	YES		YES		YES

These warnings of illnesses tied to drugs are again statistical. Table 11 shows increased *risks* from certain drugs, not sure-fire certainty. Please don't tell your child that if he uses LSD, he will become psychotic. That is not the case for the majority of kids who trip. If you argue otherwise, you will only undermine your credibility. Tell your child that *the risk for psychosis is greater* if a kid does trip than if he doesn't. Also, each psychiatric illness is likely to have many partial causes. Seldom is there one cause that "made him do it."

Avoiding drugs is like wearing a seatbelt. Do seatbelts save lives? Of course they do. But do they *always* save lives? Of course not, because other factors enter the picture, like drunk drivers, auto design, etc. Similarly, does drug abuse contribute to mental illness? Absolutely. But other factors do as well, like emotional trauma, brain injuries, infections and — as I've discussed in earlier chapters — genes! The important point, though, is that drug use and mental illness are linked. Heads-up Parenting means spotting these links to emotional disorders before too much damage has been done.

Among the more common links which parents must look out for are:

Depression

Since 1995 the number of teenaged suicides has tripled, to 2,500 a year, the third commonest cause of death among youngsters between fifteen and twenty-four. Psychiatrists look for at least five signs lingering for at least two weeks before making a diagnosis. The acronym that people use to characterize major league depression is **SIGECAPSSS.**

- **S**ad. Also blue, down in the dumps, seldom laughing or smiling, sighing a lot without reason. The kid who is spending much too much time staring at his shoe and not enough time at his homework.
- **I**nterest, the loss of it. A kid who is no longer hanging out with friends or hasn't turned his computer on in weeks.
- **G**uilt, shame or low self-esteem, when there is no reason for it.
- **E**nergy, lack of it. The kid who spends too much time in bed and has increasing trouble starting his day.
- **C**oncentration, lack of. The kid who reports having increasing trouble focusing in class or getting assignments done, especially big ones.
- **A**ppetite, usually lack of, with weight loss, though a kid can also go the other way with bingeing and weight gain.
- **P**sychomotor retardation or agitation. That is, a kid who is moving too slowly for normal or is so agitated she can't sit still.

- Sleep disturbance, either too much or too little, but a departure from what you'd expect from your kid.
- Sexual interest, lack of. Self-evident in any depressed teenager with a normal endocrine system.
- Suicidal thinking. Kids don't have to try it. They just have to talk about it to qualify.

Needless to say, suicidal thinking is the biggest flag in a depressed kid. The parent's job is to intervene before talk of trying suicide becomes reality. As I have said before, your home is not a mental hospital. And diagnosis in kids is trickier. Often they don't have many of the symptoms I've just cited at the same time. And with your kid's life on the line, you are not likely to be operating at your rock steady best. So get help! Don't try to intervene alone. Call in a professional if you think your kid has suicidal indications, don't wait, pick up the telephone today.

Psychosis

A psychotic kid is irrational. No, not in the way normal kids are. Really irrational: Believing things that simply aren't true, hearing them and, rarely, seeing them. Paranoid thinking is common. In a kid it's often unfounded fears of attack, arrest or verbal assault. An onset over hours suggests a drug like pot or cocaine, which will clear in a day or two. An onset over days and weeks is a deeper problem. Psychotic kids do crazy things in response to crazy ideas. You learn this by talking to your child. If he is making you nervous or afraid by not making sense, it's time to bring in reinforcements, namely, a psychiatrist who is experienced in treating psychosis.

Panic

These are terrible attacks of fear, often without explanation. A kid may literally feel as if he or she is going to die in the next minute, lose control somehow or go crazy. A kid's heart is likely to pound wildly. She may look like she's seen a ghost. She may tremble, gasp for breath or want to run away from the scene. These attacks last from minutes to hours. They can be stopped with the right medication.

HPPD

This is short for hallucinogen persisting perception disorder. HPPD is a chronic disturbance of vision caused by LSD-type drugs and made worse by marijuana. It consists of constant visual disturbances, including dots in the air, flashes of light, trails after moving objects and afterimages. In some unlucky kids, it can be permanent. A medical consultation is needed to rule out worse causes and get help with managing the condition. Reread chapter 8 for more information on HPPD.

Cognitive Disorders

These are problems in thinking, planning, remembering and problem solving because of substance abuse. The lucky kids are those in whom these problems clear with sobriety. Those kids with chronic alcohol use run the risk of widespread loss in mental function, alcoholic dementia. Marijuana has been known to decrease mental function, resulting in what used to be called the "amotivational syndrome." But taking any drug for an extended period would "amotivate" anyone and happily, stopping pot is usually followed by a recovery of function.

Why the First Stop for a Double Trouble Kid Should Be a Psychiatrist

Each of these diagnoses requires a "professional assessment." A frequent problem a parent has is finding the right person. There are any number of gifted professionals able to deal with drug abuse (drug and school counselors, social workers, psychologists, among others: see the discussion on *The Good Therapist* in chapter 16). However, if you suspect you have a Double Trouble kid, then you need to find a psychiatrist, preferably one experienced in kids and drugs. Failing that, then one experienced with at least one of them. Your pediatrician can help with a referral. One often overlooked source of help is your local medical society. Many are online. Most list specialties of their members, along with addresses and phone numbers. Recommendation from a parent who's already been there is also valuable.

Double Trouble kids are harder to diagnose and treat than kids who are suffering from either mental illness or substance abuse alone. Psychiatrists are especially trained in the diagnosis and treatment of mental illness, including their medical and drug related causes. They are especially trained in the use of medications, which in selected cases can be life saving.

Unfortunately, even inside hospitals, staffs for psychiatric and drug disorders are often separate. The danger is when one of the two problems is treated while the other is ignored. Parents need to insist that both problems be addressed. However, be aware that if a child is psychotic, she will not be ready to engage in the intensely cognitive and emotional work required for recovery from cocaine until the psychosis clears. First things first.

When only one problem is attended to, the other problems may go untreated, as in Janet's case. She was hospitalized for depression, given antidepressants and sent home. No one thought to ask Janet or her parents about the girl's possible drug abuse. Only after Janet continued to steal her mother's sleeping pills and overdosed on both these and her antidepressants, was this problem uncovered.

But drug use can often mask an underlying psychiatric problem. Renner was treated for alcohol abuse for a number of years from the age of sixteen. No one thought to assess if there was more to his swinging moods than episodic drunkenness. Only in his late twenties did a clinician first make the diagnosis of a debilitating bipolar disorder. By then, treatment for this disorder had been delayed unnecessarily for years.

Such cases illustrate why, if your child has a drug problem, you must have the possibility of psychiatric illness investigated and if the child has a psychiatric illness, you must ask about drugs.

Take-Home Lesson #19

1) Kids who heavily use drugs may have clouded mental states which covers underlying psychiatric problems.
2) Nine out of ten kids with drug problems have psychiatric problems needing attention. Have any drug abusing kid evaluated psychiatrically, ideally, after one month of being clean, unless the kid needs emergency measures.

3) Kids with depressive, panic, schizophrenic or bipolar disorders are at increased risk for drug abuse. If your kid carries one of these burdens, switch on your parent's radar to search for possible drug abuse.

4) The drug most closely linked to psychiatric illness is nicotine. If you fight the battle over cigarettes, you can reduce drug use later.

5) The first stop for kids with mental illness and substance abuse should be a good psychiatrist, preferably one experienced with kids and drugs.

Chapter 20

How To Make
The Drug Abuse Epidemic History

"Treatment? Where's treatment?" the federal drug czar demands in the Academy Award-winning film, *Traffic*. He's reviewing what the government does in the War on Drugs. The czar happens also to be a parent of a teenager. He is also unaware that his daughter is slipping into addiction at prep school. This is Hollywood, but even a casual reading of the daily papers tells you that it's also reality. No family is immune to the burdens of drug abuse and drug addiction. And worse, the Federal commitment to drug treatment is elusive not only in Hollywood's eyes, but in reality. The idea of the War on Drugs is simple: reducing the supply of drugs will reduce usage. However, the War has made little headway against the global 400 billion dollar illegal drug industry. Instead, demand has skyrocketed in the marketplace.

What has the War done lately? Here are a few attention getters.

- **Effect on drug use:** The effect has been little, none or a worsening of drug use. Global production, trafficking and use of marijuana, cocaine, amphetamines, heroin and Ecstasy, according to the United Nations Office of Drug Control and Crime Prevention, have all increased. The

United States remains the world's largest user of cocaine. In 2001, college student drinking in the United States continued to kill 1,445 kids a year or four kids a day. On a happier note, cocaine use in "the last twelve months" among high school seniors has declined over the last fifteen years from 12 to 6 percent. This does not appear to be due to reduced supplies, despite the War efforts, since nearly 50 percent of these students still report that cocaine is "fairly easy" or "very easy" to get. Rather, my bet is that this important drop is a result of education in the classroom and media on the harmfulness of the drug.

- **Effects on the judicial system:** Harsher laws against drug possession and sales have swamped the courts and prisons, making prisons America's fastest growing industry of the last decade. Two million people are in jail in America. The majority are there for drug related offenses. Drug offenders in the state prison system have increased nationally by 1200 percent in the last two decades. Twelve million Americans have been arrested for marijuana use. The cost, for instance, to New York State to manage its share of this law is $700,000,000 a year.

- **Effects on drug abusers:** The War has criminalized the sick and raised profit margins for drug dealers. The possession of crack today is punished far more harshly than the possession of crystalline cocaine. The result: identical chemicals in different communities put people of color in jail for longer sentences than whites. Three-strike laws, in which a repeat offender receives an automatic maximum sentence on the third offense, are most repressive for the drug-afflicted person. The nature of addiction is to compulsively repeat the "offense." One homeless addict in California received a twenty-five-year sentence for stealing a bottle of vitamins. The War on Drugs has merely piled Federal punishments of addicts on top of state punishments. The net result is to withdraw Federal funds for persons even tangentially associated with drugs, including the loss of food stamps, subsidized housing and college loans. The result has been to increase the number of people who are hungry, homeless and uneducated.

- **Effects on the Third World:** Much of the War's budget is directed toward foreign military forces, American advisors, international drug interdiction, crop spraying and diversion programs. In the name of drug abuse prevention, the United States has been advancing a policy of arming our "allies" without public debate. A recent budget for the government's drug control program reflects this approach perfectly with its mention of "relapse prevention" once, but "helicopter" fifteen times. By comparison, the budget of the Federal National Institute on Drug Abuse, one of the planet's more pre-eminent drug abuse research program, is 3 percent the size of the rest of the War budget. The War on Drugs is a nineteen-billion-dollar-a-year hammer aimed at pounding dealers and users at home and abroad. The effect on policy is clear: if you only have a hammer, then every addict is a nail.

Feeling Helpless?

Don't. The drug problem is your problem, our problem. We can solve it together. It takes knowledge. Reading this book will give you a jump on the issues. Solutions take commitment. But you must act. Even little actions can lead to big results.

Remember the tragic death of Chuck in chapter 8 who died of alcohol poisoning after he was locked in a trunk during a fraternity hazing. It's likely that helplessness was one of a welter of feelings experienced by Chuck's parents on the news of his death. His mom, Eileen Stevens, had no particular expertise in alcohol, drugs or fraternity hazing at the time. But she learned fast, overcoming barriers to the truth put up by the fraternity and the boy's university. Her work exposed the despicable practice of college hazing that took her son's life and the institutions that looked the other way. It also led to the film *Broken Pledges* and the passage of anti-hazing laws in forty-two states. Hazing still involves nearly two million teenagers in the United States each year. Drug and alcohol abuse are still a part of it, but Eileen Stevens has to be counted as a Heads-up Parent who made a difference.

Dads can make a difference as well. Consider the story of Gary Langis, a modern Enemy of the People. The Ibsen play of the same name is about Dr. Thomas Stockmann, a doctor in a small town who discovers that the water in the town baths, a big tourist attraction, is contaminated. Stockmann is a guy who can't keep his mouth shut and in his efforts to save his town, he becomes labeled an "enemy of the people." Unlike Stockmann, Gary Langis didn't go to medical school. But he knew that AIDS and hepatitis C were being spread in his community of Revere, Massachusetts by addicts using contaminated needles. Langis is a parent and grandparent. AIDS had already struck down his wife. And so in 1989 he started giving addicts sterile needles in exchange for their used ones. The idea was straightforward. An addict shooting drugs with clean equipment is far less likely to become infected than one sharing the stuff with another addict and less likely to spread viral diseases to the rest of the community.

The idea was controversial. Some community leaders feared that a needle exchange program would bring criminal elements to town. Some held the mistaken belief that clean needles would promote addiction, as if kids were saying, "There's a needle exchange program in town. I think I'll use heroin." Many research groups, including our own, had shown, on the other hand, that one of the biggest risk factors for transmitting viral infections like AIDS and hepatitis C is the sharing of injection equipment. In other words, needle exchange programs among addicts are the equivalent of safe sex in the prevention of AIDS and hepatitis C. An added benefit of such programs is that addicts seeking clean needles are also opening the door to medical treatment and recovery.

The city of Lynn, Massachusetts, objected. On February 1, 2001 Langis was arrested and charged with possession and distribution of syringes. This was despite the lawful status of needle exchange in a handful of other Massachusetts cities. His case went to trial, where Langis told the jury, "Our mission is completely clear, that we will provide sterile injection equipment to at-risk populations, no matter what ZIP code they live in." The jury got the message. They didn't want more AIDS or hepatitis in their community, either. Langis was acquitted.

Langis is not alone. Hawaii has a statewide needle exchange program. It also cut the rate of HIV infection among needle users by 80 percent in five years. At least twenty-five states now fund needle exchange. A study of eighty-one cities around the world found lower HIV infection rates among needle users in cities that had exchange programs than cities that did not. This is harm reduction at its best. It is also a sensible public health policy.

Some federal programs are not so sensible or successful, such as Plan Columbia, which seeks to spend 1.3 billion dollars of the War on Drugs budget on training and equipping what the New York Times calls "counternarcotics battalions" in that war torn country. Coca crops and parts of the rainforest are now defoliated with the chemical glyphosate as a result of drug reduction policies. On the way to ending the drug epidemic, our government has gotten lost. It's our job to get things on track. Our objective should be prevention and treatment.

Dr. Lonny Shavelson cites a RAND study in his excellent book on addicts, *Hooked,* which found that for every twenty-three dollars spent abroad to reduce drug production, the same effect in reducing cocaine consumption would be achieved by spending one dollar in drug treatment at home. This is appalling, because it underscores the waste in current efforts to reduce drug supply. It is also hopeful, because it means we can do so much more in treatment. The trend in the past few years has been in the wrong direction. Witness the story of Vietnam veteran Ibrahim Akram, who after a lifetime of drug addiction, was first able to get treatment at the age of sixty. He's from Ohio, where there are an estimated 75,000 people in state-sponsored treatment programs among an estimated *million* people who need them. Worse, cuts in Federal support are being translated into cuts in treatment.

But since the Federal government has dropped the ball, what can one father or mother do? The short answer is lots. Here is a short list of actions parents can take individually and in groups. The longer list is the one you will come up with after looking around your community. You can change things with a letter, a phone call, a petition, a vote. They all count.

- Insist that your child attend schools and colleges with strict no-drug policies and ask the college about their policy before your kid applies
- Reduce and restrict local alcohol and cigarette advertisements
- Improve (or start) effective, science-based programs of drug education in schools

- Expand physician involvement in smoke cessation efforts
- Work to improve insurance coverage to treat nicotine addiction
- Increase taxes on smokers, tobacco growers and cigarette manufacturers
- Support investigations into cigarette smuggling
- Support conversion of tobacco farming into responsible farming
- Support public funding of smoke cessation courses
- Expand alcohol and smoke-free zones in your town
- Promote zero smoking tolerance in high schools
- Support mandatory education of minors found with cigarettes and alcohol
- Require package-labeling of cigarettes to say more explicitly what tobacco does to the smoker
- Support public funding of alcohol abstinence programs
- Work for a ban of direct patient marketing of prescription drugs
- Never underestimate the power of common sense

I add this last statement after learning of a high school principal in 2003 who acted on a tip that certain kids were dealing drugs in school. His response was to hide the police in closets and stairwells and then have over a hundred kids rounded up with the use of drawn guns, handcuffs and a drug-sniffing dog and forcing them to kneel and face the wall. The majority of students in the school are white. The majority of the kids arrested were black. No drugs were found. No kids were charged. This story speaks volumes about our problems with drugs, race and the sense of panic of which a community is capable when trying to deal with these complicated issues. It also shows what a shortage of common sense can lead to. Fortunately, for every dumb idea about stopping drug abuse there are ten good ones.

Some other areas to work on are universal health insurance and insurance parity for substance abuse treatment with other medical care. I know. You're probably thinking that these issues are *huge and how in the world could parents ever make a difference in these areas by themselves.* You're right. You can't do this alone. You need

reinforcements. You need power. Here is how to get it:
1) Get informed.
2) Get active.
3) Get organized.
4) Get noticed.
5) Get political.

Getting Informed

This book is a beginning. It does not have all the answers. As a rule of thumb, never rely on a single source of information, but test multiple sources against each other to draw meaningful conclusions. Certainly, it would be a mistake to rely on only one source of information on a subject as complex as the drug epidemic. The Internet is a treasure trove of information on drugs. It also can be a stinky swamp of misinformation from crackpots, cults and lunatics. Chapter 16 discusses how to sort this out.

My favorite source of drug information comes from PubMed, the free database of the world's medical literature organized by the National Library of Medicine. You can find it at *http://www.ncbi.nlm.nih.gov/-entrez/query.fcgi*. These are scientific papers, however and may make for slow going. More user friendly are websites run by the National Institutes on Drug Abuse (NIDA, found at *http://www.nida.nih.gov/*) and the PrevLine service of the Substance Abuse and Mental Health Services Administration (SAMHSA, found at (*http://www.health.org/*). A good parent advocacy group is the Partnership for a Drug-Free America (*http://www.drugfreeamerica.org/*).

Remember that in drug abuse it is extremely difficult for anyone to avoid bias. We are each conditioned by our experiences and drugs create more than enough experiences to go around. A parent who looks fondly on his days as a marijuana user at Woodstock will feel differently about drugs from a parent who was hospitalized as a teen for a psychotic break following LSD. To a great extent drug scholars and advocates, even if educated to shun bias, will be vulnerable to the same forces. A good question to ask about any source of information is what the social agenda is likely to be of that source. That doesn't automatically invalidate the source, but tread cautiously.

Getting Active

Reach out to your friends, neighbors and other parents to find out what the problems are in your community and think through possible solutions. Meet regularly, meet often and keep the talk focused on the topic. You are informing each other at this stage and trying on different approaches for size. Set flexible goals.

Don't be rigid, however. Your goals are likely to change. You may decide that trying to raise the legal drinking age (a good idea!) will save lives in your state, but a new campaign against teen smoking may give you more results sooner. Find people with a passion for the problem with whom to work. Good things will come of it.

Getting Organized

Once you have assembled a group of people around an idea, you have the beginnings of an organization, just like MADD, SADD, AA and the alphabet soup of like-minded organizations. Indeed, working through one of them may suit your temperament more than starting your own organization, but it you must, you must. It just takes time, zeal, patience, knowledge, charm and charisma. A little money won't hurt, either, though too much money, contrary to popular misconception, will hurt you, since the goal of your organization is to promote a vision, not to degenerate into a nest of accountants.

Organizations promoting social change often seek recognition as non-profit (501c3) corporations. Good idea! This makes the organization tax exempt. Donations are tax deductible. Your group can get breaks on postal rates and access to a variety of public governmental agencies. The organization can even make a profit, providing it's the organization and not private individuals, which benefits from the organization's growth. To achieve this, you have to demonstrate to the IRS that the money that comes to you through donations, dues and the like is dedicated to a specific pre-defined mission.

So now that I made a non-profit corporation sound like Heaven for movers and shakers, the Devil is still in the details. A non-profit is *not* allowed to electioneer in support of any candidate for any political office. You can lobby for legislation or referenda on the ballot, but only at a rate of less than 20 percent of your budget per year. Breaking these rules risks losing your tax-exempt status.

You might imagine that the non-profit rules essentially muzzle you from speaking up about anything "political." Not so. Specifically permitted are activities related to public education if they are nonpartisan, objective and fairly consider alternative points of view. Many issues regarding drugs and health are clearly bipartisan in nature. Giving expert or viewpoint testimony to legislatures is not considered lobbying. Neither is using unpaid volunteers. Clearly, there is an art to this. You learn it as you go along. There are a busload of folks with non-profit experience who have been there who can give you guidance in these matters. Many probably are in your own community.

I tend to see non-profit organizations as two types: paper-based organizations and member-based ones. Both do a job. The paper organizations are better than they sound. You probably belong to one or two of them. A paper organization is one that has a mission, builds a paper membership, collects dues and promotes its vision of public policy through education. Members may get educational newsletters or journals in return.

The Union of Concerned Scientists is a good example of a paper-based organization. It delivers high profile messages such as its World Scientists' Warning To Humanity, which was signed by over 1500 prestigious academicians in 1992. Signers included many Nobel Prize winners. Such groups help, but the limitation of a paper group is that it depends on the action of the few on behalf of the many. No matter how lofty the status of the few or inspired their message, the signers for the most part do not often leave their laboratories to rush to the service of a mission. This brings us to the second type of organization, the member-based one.

Member-based groups might want you to march in the streets and barricade the offices of your legislators. But they usually don't say so. Instead, members take on the issues more civilly. They are often chapter-based, which facilitates grassroots activism. They run on some money and a lot of sweat. The Sierra Club is a good example of this type of organization. MADD also does this well, with multiple chapters in each state. (MADD also has a strong national leadership.) Member organizations don't have to tackle policy issues to be effective. Alcoholics Anonymous, Al-Anon and Alateen typify member organizations that help people directly with scant interest in public policy. They're people-to-people, hands on, in the trenches type folks where you only get what you need by showing up. They can have a huge effect. Alanon has 24,000 groups worldwide. Both paper-based and member-based organizations are effective. But there is one requirement for that to happen: you have to get noticed.

Getting Noticed

Building a group and educating people is the goal. A number of doctors and I did this when we formed Physicians for Social Responsibility. What began as an idea of MIT psychiatrist Eric Chivian became a series of national symposia on the medical consequences of nuclear war, which led to a national organization, an international one and eventually the Nobel Peace Prize, which I shared in 1985.

There were many elements to this success story: inspirational leaders such as Helen Caldicott and Bernard Lown and an army of dedicated physicians around the world willing to direct their energies to this work. Another element was the presentation of medical information to the media that was fresh and important, in the form of studies, press releases, lectures, television and radio interviews and op-ed pieces. Creativity counts as well, like that of the physician who attempted to draw media attention to the problem of increased teen smoking by dressing like a giant cigarette. Needless to say, it worked. The drug epidemic is a natural issue in this regard, since new important data arrive at the doorsteps of the media nearly daily.

Drawing media attention to your work builds membership and legislative sensitivity to the issue. Apply the pulse test. What problem about young people abusing drugs makes your heart skip a beat? Passion is critical. Look around your community. What is the legal drinking age? Should it be raised? It would reduce teenage driving deaths. (Remember to credit kids with common sense when you see it. Kids can be important allies. A survey of 514 teens in 2001 discovered that 68 percent favored a legal drinking age of twenty-one and 16 percent more favored raising it.) What about smoking cessation programs? These are issues where finding other parents with similar feelings comes into play. You multiply your power by creating an organization and building membership. Then you can take on bigger targets.

Get Political

If you are thinking now that this is an invitation to get political, you're right. Political is not a four-letter word. You can make a difference, as surely as the beating of a butterfly's wings in California can cause a tornado in Indonesia (at least according to the mathematics of chaos theory). Improve the drug laws of your state. Your weapons can be simply a telephone, a personal computer and a kitchen table. A few ideas you may want to think about include:

- Federal funding for rural residential programs
- Federal funding for methadone maintenance and needle exchange programs
- Federal support of residential treatment services
- Repeal of laws depriving addicts of housing, food and educational benefits
- Decriminalize the marijuana laws
- End racial discrimination in cocaine laws

Remember, our goal in making the epidemic of drug abuse history is to replace punishment with prevention and treatment. The future of this enterprise is in our hands and no others. Small changes that we make may be immediate and long-lived. Larger changes are in our reach as well, with hard work and patience. Now is the time to start. As the mandarin advised the gardner, if the tree will not bloom for a hundred years, plant it today.

Take-Home Lesson #20

1) Turn the ineffective drug war into a positive campaign of prevention and treatment.
2) Get informed, active, organized, noticed and political.
3) Start making changes in your neighborhood and community.
4) Start today.